麦格希 **中英双语阅读文库**

世界经典散文集

【美】琳恩·富尔顿 (Lynn Fulton) ● 主编

刘慧 ● 译

麦格希中英双语阅读文库编委会 ● 编

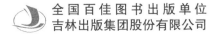

全国百佳图书出版单位
吉林出版集团股份有限公司

图书在版编目（CIP）数据

世界经典散文集 / (美) 琳恩·富尔顿
(Lynn Fulton) 主编；麦格希中英双语阅读文库编委会
编；刘慧译. -- 2版. -- 长春：吉林出版集团股份有
限公司, 2018.3（2022.1重印）
（麦格希中英双语阅读文库）
ISBN 978-7-5581-4786-9

Ⅰ.①世… Ⅱ.①琳… ②麦… ③刘… Ⅲ.①英语—
汉语—对照读物②散文集—世界 Ⅳ.①H319.4：I

中国版本图书馆CIP数据核字(2018)第045970号

世界经典散文集

| 编：麦格希中英双语阅读文库编委会
插　　画：齐　航　李延霞
责任编辑：孙琳琳
封面设计：冯冯翼
开　　本：660mm × 960mm　1/16
字　　数：167千字
印　　张：10
版　　次：2018年3月第2版
印　　次：2022年1月第2次印刷

出　　版：吉林出版集团股份有限公司
发　　行：吉林出版集团外语教育有限公司
地　　址：长春市福祉大路5788号龙腾国际大厦B座7层
　　　　　邮编：130011
电　　话：总编办：0431-81629929
　　　　　发行部：0431-81629927　0431-81629921(Fax)
印　　刷：北京一鑫印务有限责任公司

ISBN 978-7-5581-4786-9　　　定价：36.00元
版权所有　　侵权必究　　举报电话：0431-81629929

前 言 *PREFACE*

英国思想家培根说过：阅读使人深刻。阅读的真正目的是获取信息，开拓视野和陶冶情操。从语言学习的角度来说，学习语言若没有大量阅读就如隔靴搔痒，因为阅读中的语言是最丰富、最灵活、最具表现力、最符合生活情景的，同时读物中的情节、故事引人入胜，进而能充分调动读者的阅读兴趣，培养读者的文学修养，至此，语言的学习水到渠成。

"麦格希中英双语阅读文库"在世界范围内选材，涉及科普、社会文化、文学名著、传奇故事、成长励志等多个系列，充分满足英语学习者课外阅读之所需，在阅读中学习英语、提高能力。

◎难度适中

本套图书充分照顾读者的英语学习阶段和水平，从读者的阅读兴趣出发，以难易适中的英语语言为立足点，选材精心、编排合理。

◎精品荟萃

本套图书注重经典阅读与实用阅读并举。既包含国内外脍炙人口、耳熟能详的美文，又包含科普、人文、故事、励志类等多学科的精彩文章。

◎功能实用

本套图书充分体现了双语阅读的功能和优势，充分考虑到读者课外阅读的方便，超出核心词表的词汇均出现在使其意义明显的语境之中，并标注释义。

鉴于编者水平有限，凡不周之处，谬误之处，皆欢迎批评教正。

我们真心地希望本套图书承载的文化知识和英语阅读的策略对提高读者的英语著作欣赏水平和英语运用能力有所裨益。

丛书编委会

Contents

January Wind

—— *Hal Borland*

The January wind has a hundred voices. It can scream, it can bellow, it can whisper, and it can sing a *lullaby*. It can roar throught the leafless oaks and shout down the hillside, and it can murmur in the white pines rooted among the *granite ledges* where *lichen* makes strange hieroglyphics. It can

---

冬 风 破

——[美] 哈尔·伯兰德

月的风有着上百种声音。它时而尖叫，时而咆哮，时而低语，时而轻吟。有时它穿过萧索的橡树，一路呼啸掠过山岗，在布满地衣的岩石上，与白雪覆盖的松树窃窃私语。而有时它又吹着口哨钻进烟囱，与壁炉里的火共舞。若是在阳光灿烂的日子，它会停下脚步，躲进角落，低声许下春与紫罗兰的承诺。在冰冷孤寂的夜晚，它会沙沙地敲过

---

lullaby *n.* 摇篮曲；催眠曲
ledge *n.* 岩架

granite *n.* 花岗岩；花岗石
lichen *n.* 地衣

whistle down a chimney and set the hearth-flames to dancing. On a sunny day it can pause in a sheltered spot and breathe a promise of spring and violets. In the cold of a lonely night it can *rattle* the *sash* and stay there muttering of ice and snowbanks and deep-frozen pond.

Sometimes the January wind seems to come from the farthest star in the outer darkness, so remote and so *impersonal* is its voice. That is the wind of a January dawn, in the half-light that trembles between day and night. It is a wind that merely quivers the trees, its force sensed but not seen, a force that might almost hold back the day if it were so directed. Then the east brightens, and the wind relaxes—the stars, its source, grown *dim*.

And sometimes the January wind is so intimate that you know it came only from the next hill, a little wind that plays with leaves and

---

格窗，描述外面的冰天雪地，还有冰冻的池塘。

有的时候，一月的风似乎从那无际幽暗中最远的那颗星上飞来，那声音，是如此遥远、如此冷漠。这是一月黎明的风，在暗夜与白天交错的微光中怒吼着。这是让树木也随之颤抖的风。它的力量，虽然看不见但却感觉得到。那是一股可以阻止时间前进的力量。接着东方渐明，风渐渐地弱了下去，而被看作风的源头的那颗远星在渐亮的天色中缓缓隐去。

然而有的时候，那一月的风是如此得亲近，仿佛就来自附近的那座小山。微风轻拂，抚弄青青嫩叶，追逐袅袅炊烟；风声轻扬，宛若撅着嘴的小男

---

rattle *v.* （使）发出格格的响声
impersonal *adj.* 不受个人情感影响的；冷淡的

sash *n.* 窗扇
dim *adj.* 模糊的；看不清楚的

puffs at chimney smoke and whistles like a little boy with *puckered* lips. It makes the little *cedar* trees quiver, as with delight. It shadow-boxes with the weather vane. It *tweaks* an ear, and whispers laughing words about *crocuses* and daffodils, and nips the nose and dances off.

But you never know, until you hear its voice, which wind is here today.

Or, more important, which will be here tomorrow.

孩儿吹着口哨。它让雪松欣然起舞，它捉弄着可怜的风向标，让它不停地旋转，偶尔还拉住行人的耳朵，诉说关于番红花和黄水仙的有趣故事，然后捏一捏他的鼻子，蹦跳着远去。

但是你若不曾听到它的声响，就不会知道，今天吹着的风，是凛冽冷漠的还是温和亲近的。

或者，更重要的是，明天会吹什么风。

---

pucker *v.* 撅起　　　　　　　　　　cedar *n.* 雪松
tweak *v.* 拧；捏；扭　　　　　　　crocus *n.* 番红花

Morning Light

—*Charles Dickens*

The town was glad with morning light; places that had shown ugly and *distrustful* all night long, now wore a smile; and sparking *sunbeams* dancing on *chamber* windows, and twinkling through blind and curtain before sleepers' eyes, shed light even into dreams, and chased away the shadows of the night. Birds

---

曙光普照
——［英］查尔斯·狄更斯

因为晨曦，整个镇子都欢乐起来。夜里丑陋可疑的地方也都泛起了笑容。闪烁的日光在卧室的窗子上跳跃，透过窗帘与帐幔闪耀在眠者的眼睛上，照耀进他们的梦里，赶走夜的幽暗。暖房里的小鸟儿，虽然在幽暗中被关得紧紧的，也感觉到了清晨的来临，于是在小小的笼子里不 安分起来；有着晶晶亮眼睛的小老鼠爬回洞里，怯生生地缩在

---

distrustful *adj.* 不信任的；怀疑的；可疑的　　sunbeam *n.* 阳光光束；快乐的人
chamber *n.* 房间

in hot rooms, covered up closed and dark, felt it was morning, and chafed and grew restless in their little cells; bright-eyed mice crept back to their ting homes and nestled timidly together; the sleek house-cat, forgetful of her prey, sat winking at the rays of sun starting through *keyhole* and *cranny* in the door, and longed for her stealthy run and warm sleek bask outside. The nobler beasts confined in dens stood motionless behind their bars, and gazed on fluttering boughs and sunshine peeping through some little window, with eyes in which old forests gleamed—then trod impatiently the track their prisoned feet had worn—and stopped and gazed again. Men in their dungeons stretched their cramp cold limbs and cursed the stone that no bright sky could warm. The flowers that sleep by night, opened their gentle eyes and turned them to the day. The light, creation's mind, was everywhere, and all things owned its power.

一起；滑溜溜的家猫早把猎物抛在脑后，在阳光下眯着眼睛，望着从钥匙孔和门缝中射进来的光，渴望着溜到外面去。马厩里高贵的生物，静静地立在木栏后面，一动不动，凝视着摇晃的树与小窗子透进来的阳光，眼中仿佛藏着一片老树林，继而不耐烦地践踏着它们自己踏出来的蹄窝，然后又安静下来凝视。牢狱里的人们伸展着冰冷的四肢，咒骂这身下连晴朗的天气也暖不过来的石头。夜里的睡花张开了温柔的眼睛，抬起头来望着白昼。每一个角落都洒满了光亮，那是造物主的光辉，万事万物都拥有了它的力量。

---

keyhole *n.* 锁眼；钥匙孔   cranny *n.* 裂缝；缝隙

3

August

——Charles Dickens

There is no month in the whole year, in which nature wears a more beautiful appearance than in the month of August.

Spring has many beauties, and May is a fresh and blooming month, but the *charms* of this time of year are enhanced by their contrast with the winter season. August has no such advantage. It comes

八月之美

—— [英]查尔斯·狄更斯

一年之中，大自然最美的月份莫过于八月了。

春天固然有许多动人之处，五月也确是明媚清新，繁花似锦的月份，但其魅力却是通过与冬天的对比而凸显出来的。八月可没有这样的优势。它来时我们记得的只有晴天、绿野与香花。而冰雪与寒风早已从我们的记忆中完全褪去，如同它们从地球上消失那样了无声息。呵！八月，

charm *n.* 魅力；吸引力

when we remember nothing but clear skies, green fields, and sweet—smelling flowers—when the recollection of snow, and ice, and *bleak* winds, has faded from our minds as completely as they have disappeared from the earth—and yet what a pleasant time it is!

Orchards and cornfields ring with the *hum* of labours; trees bend beneath the thick *clusters* of rich fruit which bow their branches to the ground; and the corn, piled in graceful sheaves, or waving in every light breath that sweeps above it, as if it wooed the sickle, tinges the landscape with a golden hue.

A mellow softness appears to hang over the whole earth; the influence of the season seems to extend itself to the very wagon, whose slow motion across the well-reaped field, is perceptible only to the eye, but strikes with no harsh sound upon the ear.

多可爱的季节！

　　果园与谷地里回荡着忙碌劳作的声响。结着硕果的枝条像是要垂到了地面。而谷子呢，有的被整整齐齐地堆着，有的正迎风招展，仿佛在向镰刀求爱。它们为这田野染上了金色的光晕。

　　一种温柔丰美的气息笼罩着大地。就连马车都仿佛受到了感染。秋收完毕的田野，一辆马车缓慢而行，听不到任何忙碌喧嚣，而我们的眼睛却领略了安静之美。

---

bleak *adj.* 阴冷的；阴郁的；凄凉的　　　　orchard *n.* （通常指围起来的）果园
hum *n.* 嗡嗡声　　　　　　　　　　　　　cluster *n.* （果实、花等的）串；簇

Night

—Nathaniel Hawthovne

Night has fallen over the country. Through the trees rises the red moon and the stars are scarcely seen. In the vast shadow of night the coolness and the dews descend. I sit at the open window to enjoy them; and hear only the voice of the summer wind. Like black *hulks*, the shadows of the great trees ride at *anchor* on the *billowy* sea of grass. I

夜幕降临

—— [美]纳撒尼尔·霍桑

夜幕已经降临,笼罩着山村。树林后面冉冉升起一轮红月,几乎看不到星星。夜色苍茫,寒气与露水渐渐地降下来。我坐在窗前欣赏着这夜景,窗户开着,耳边只听到那夏的风声。大树的阴影落在茫茫草地上,就像黑色的大船停泊在波浪起伏的海上。虽然我看不到红色和蓝色的花儿,但我知道它们就在那儿。远处的草地上,银色的查尔斯河闪

hulk *n.* 笨重的大船   anchor *n.* 锚
billowy *adj.* 巨浪似的;汹涌的

cannot see the red and blue flowers, but I know that they are there. Far away in the meadow gleams the silver Charles. The *tramp* of horses' *hoofs* sounds from the wooden bridge. Then all is still save the continuous wind of the summer night. Sometimes I know not if it be the wind or the sound of the neighboring sea. The village clock strikes; and I feel that I am not alone.

How different it is in the city! It is late, and the crowd is gone. You step out upon the balcony, and lie in the very *bosom* of the cool, dewy night as if you folded her *garments* about you. Beneath lies the public walk with trees, like a fathomless, black gulf, into whose silent darkness the spirit plunges, and float away with some beloved spirit clasped in its embrace. The lamps are still burning up and down the long street. People go by with grotesque shadows, now foreshortened, and now lengthening away into the darkness and

---

闪发光。马蹄声踢踢踏踏地从木桥那边传来。接着，万物俱寂，只留下夏夜不绝的风声。有时，我丝毫辨不出那究竟是风声，还是近处的海声。这个时候，村子里的钟敲起来了，于是我觉得并不孤单。

城市的夜晚是多么得不同啊！夜深人散。走上阳台，躺在清凉、露水浸润的夜幕中，仿佛是将这夜色作为外衣裹住了身体。阳台下面的林荫人行道，像一条深不可测的黑色海湾，飘忽的精灵就投入了这静默的黑暗之中，然后拥抱着某个所爱的精灵随波而去。长长的大街上，街灯依然亮着。人们从灯下走过，拖着各种各样奇形怪状的影子，影子时而缩短，时而伸长。一会儿的工夫，就消失在了黑暗中，但当行人走过路灯的一刹

---

tramp *n.* 脚步声
bosom *n.* 胸怀；内心

hoof *n.* （兽的）蹄；马蹄
garment *n.* 衣服

vanishing, while a new one springs up behind the walker, and seems to pass him revolving like the sail of a *windmill*. The iron gates of the park shut with a jangling *clang*. There are footsteps and loud voices; —a *tumult*; —a drunken *brawl*; —an alarm of fire; —then silence again. And now at length the city is asleep, and we can see the night. The belated moon looks over the roofs, and finds no one to welcome her. The moonlight is broken. It lies here and there in the squares and the opening of the streets—angular like blocks of white marble.

那，新的影子又会突然出现，这回，影子像风车上的翼板一样，"呼"地转到那人前方去了。"嘡"的一声，公园的铁门关上了。脚步声和嘈杂说话声响起，一阵喧哗，一阵酒后的吵闹，一阵火警声，然后，回归寂静。于是，城市终于睡去，我们也才终于看到了夜色。姗姗来迟的月亮从屋顶后面探出脸来，发觉没有人在欢迎她。月光碎了一地，撒落在广场上和宽阔的大街上，棱角分明得仿佛一块块白色的大理石。

---

windmill *n.* 风车；风车房
tumult *n.* 吵闹；喧哗；激动的吵闹声

clang *n.* 叮当声
brawl *n.* 争吵；打架

After a Long Winter

— Eileen O' Hara

Up earlier than usual. The air is calling. Spring air is different from winter air.

Tree branches are *serrated* with red bud teeth. Later, they grow *chartreuse fuzz*, making pale green auras in the sun. Summer leaves will be dark, shading, but spring leaves let the light through. Spring trees glow in the daytime, spreading

---

严冬过后
—— [美]艾琳·奥哈拉

这天我比往常起得要早，是因为那空气在召唤。春天的空气与冬天的比就是不一样。

树的枝丫，遍布红色嫩芽，连成了锯子状的一条条，像枝丫长的牙齿。接下来，它们会长成黄绿色的绒叶，在阳光的照耀下泛着淡绿的光辉。夏天的树叶色调是暗沉的，可是春日的叶子透着轻盈与明快。树木在春日下尽情成长，撑起半透明的华盖。

---

serrated *adj.* 锯齿状的
fuzz *n.* 绒毛；轻柔的物质

chartreuse *n.* 黄绿色

translucent canopies.

The birds are out, racketing their news from bush to branch. Cats are still curled up on fire escapes. They are in no hurry to get up in the cool morning air and they know it will warm up later. They are watching the birds. They can wait.

The air is clear, clean cool. The smells are tiny smells, little *whiffs* of green, a *ribbon* of brown mud, the blue smell of the sky. Midday is mild enough for short sleeves. I eat my lunch outside, sitting on a warm brick wall. The breeze lifts my hair and *riffles* the edge of my skirt. I have to *squint*. Everything tastes better.

Until today I had been too huddled in my winter coat to notice the quiet coming of flowers. Suddenly, daffodils smile in my face,

鸟儿纷纷出巢，忙着在丛枝间叽叽喳喳地互通消息。猫咪仍旧缩在防火梯上，并不急着在空气有些清凉的早上出来活动，因为它们知道不久过后，天才会暖和起来。它们在盯着小鸟的一举一动，等候不是问题。

空气清新、干净又凉爽，飘着淡淡的气味。微风卷过阵阵青草的迷香，也有一股棕色泥土的清新，还有天空那湛蓝的味道。中午不太热，可以穿着短袖。我坐在外面一堵晒暖的砖墙上吃着午饭。微风吹起我的发梢，裙摆随风飘舞。阳光下，我不得不眯着眼睛，但是却觉得吃什么都更可口了。

我一直把自己包裹在冬大衣里，直到今天才发觉那春日的花儿已经悄无声息地绽放了。仿佛一眨眼的工夫，水仙花已迎着我绽放笑颜，鹦鹉郁

whiff *n.* 一股（微弱的）气味
riffle *v.* （使）起涟漪；迅速翻动

ribbon *n.* 带；缎带；丝带
squint *v.* 眯着眼睛；斜着眼睛（看某物）

parrot tulips wave their *beaky* petals, and fragrant white blossoms are pinned to *dogwood* trees like bows in a young girl's hair.

The evening is soft. I need my thin jacket. It's still light out when I walk home from the Metro. I could walk for hours. Like a kid playing street games with her friends, I don't want to go in.

When I went to work this morning, I left my windows open. Spring came in through the screens while I was gone. It's as if I had used a big sliver key and rolled back the roof like a *lid* on a *sardine* can. The indoors smell like the outdoors. It will be like lying down in the grass to sleep.

The sheets are cool. The quilt is warm. The light fades outside my windows.

金香摇摆着那鸟嘴状的花瓣，而朵朵芬芳雪白的花点缀在山茱萸树枝头，像少女头上的蝴蝶结。

日色西沉，天气微凉，我得穿上薄外套。从地铁出来步行回家的时候，天还亮着。我可以像这样走上好几个小时。像小孩子喜欢流连在街头和朋友一起玩游戏那样，我也不想回到屋里去。

早上出门前，我打开窗户，这样，即使我不在家，春的气息也会透过纱窗蔓延进来。这就像是打开一个沙丁鱼罐头，我用一把超大的银色钥匙开启了我的屋顶。此刻，屋内和屋外有着相同的味道。就像躺在青草地上似的睡去。

清凉的床，被子暖暖的。光亮渐渐在窗外褪去。

---

beaky *adj.* 像鸟嘴的

lid *n.* 盖；盖子

dogwood *n.* 山茱萸

sardine *n.* 沙丁鱼（罐装的）

Autumn Sunset

— Henry David Thoreau

We had a remarkable sunset one day last November. I was walking in a *meadow*, the source of a small *brook*, when the sun at last, just before setting, after a cold gray day, reached a clear *stratum* in the horizon, and the softest, brightest morning sunlight fell on the dry grass and on the stems of the trees in the opposite horizon,

晚霞映秋
　　—— [美] 亨利·大卫·梭罗

去年十一月的一天，我们目睹了一次极其壮丽的日落。那个时候，我正漫步于草地之上，这草地是一道小溪的发源处。天际的太阳，在一个凛冽的灰蒙蒙的寒天之后，正准备落下。它涌出云层，绽放澄澈的光明，柔美且耀眼，照耀着天幕下的衰草与老枝以及山边的橡树。而我们影子也长长地延展在东边草地，仿佛是那缕余晖中仅有的点点

---

meadow　*n.* 草地；牧场　　　　　　　　　　　　brook　*n.* 小溪
stratum　*n.* 岩层；地层

and on the leaves of the shrub-oaks on the hill-side, while our shadows stretched long over the meadow eastward, as if we were the only *motes* in its *beams*. It was such a light as we could not have imagined a moment before, and the air also was so warm and *serene* that nothing wanted to make a *paradise* of that meadow. When we reflected that this was not a solitary phenomenon, never to happen again, but that it would happen forever and ever an infinite number of evenings, and cheer and reassure the latest child that walked there, it was more glorious still.

The sun sets on some retired meadow, where no house is visible, with all the glory and splendor that it lavishes on cities, and, perchance, as it has never set before, —where there is but a solitary marsh-hawk to have his wings gilded by it, or only a musquash

尘埃。这光明是那么得美好，一晌之前还是难以想象。空气温暖安详，不需要再添加什么，这草地已俨然是天堂。当我们再仔细一想，这样的情形并不是绝无仅有，后无来者的，因为它会在无数的傍晚出现，温暖着、感动着在它之中走过的上帝的孩子们。想到这里，眼前的景色就愈发显得壮丽起来。

夕阳斜映在了无人烟的草地上，同样的，它也将这余晖大方地照耀在城市，仿佛从来没有过的美丽。茫茫之中瞥见一只孤零零的沼鹰，羽翼尽染金黄，一只麝香鼠从洞穴中探头出来，一股水色黝黑的小溪正在沼泽中蜿蜒而前，绕过一堆残枝落叶。我们漫步在这纯美的光辉中，这光辉为

mote *n.* 尘埃
serene *adj.* 宁静的；安详的

beam *n.* 光线
paradise *n.* 天堂；乐土

lookout from his cabin, and there is some little black-veined brook in the midst of the marsh, just beginning to meander, winding slowly round a decaying *stump*. We walked in so pure and bright a light, gilding the withered grass and leaves, so softly and serenely bright, I thought I had never bathed in such a golden flood, without a *ripple* or a *murmur* to it. The west side of every wood and rising ground gleamed like a boundary of Elysium, and the sun on our backs seemed like a gentle *herdsman* driving us home at evening.

So we saunter toward the Holy Land, till one day the sun shall shine more brightly than ever he has done, shall perchance shine into our minds and hearts, and light up our whole lives with a great awakening light, as warm and serene and golden as on a bank-side in autumn.

残枝涂上金色，温柔又明亮。我不曾想到自己会沉浸在如此美好的光影之中，没有一丝涟漪与打扰。树林之西与那地平线交融，闪着光芒，就仿佛是那极乐之巅的边境。而身后的夕阳宛若慈祥的牧人，趁着薄暮时分，赶送我们归去。

就这样，我们向那欢乐之境蹒跚走去，直至有一天这太阳照耀得比往常更加明媚，照耀进我们的心扉灵府之中，用那唤醒的光亮照耀我们的整个生命，就像此刻河畔那金黄温暖又安详的秋天的落日。

---

stump *n.* 残余部分；残根
murmur *n.* 低语声

ripple *n.* 涟漪
herdsman *n.* 牧人

7

The Lesson of the Bamboo Trees

—— *Anonymous*

One of my fondest memories as a child is going by the river and sitting *idly* on the bank. There I would enjoy the peace and quiet, watch the water rush downstream and listen to the *chirps* of birds and the rustling of leaves in the trees. I would also watch the bamboo trees bend under pressure from the wind and watch them return

悟理于竹
—— 佚名

童年时，我最深刻的记忆就是到河边去散步，在河堤上懒散地坐着。坐在那儿，看着水奔流而下，聆听林间鸟鸣啾啾以及树叶摩挲私语，尽情享受安宁与静谧。同时，我也会观察那风中的翠竹在烈风的强劲肆虐下弯下了腰身，风停后，又仪态万方地恢复原状。

---

idly *adv.* 懒惰地；无所事事地　　　　　　　chirp *n.* 鸟叫；虫鸣

gracefully to their original position after the wind had died down.

When I think about the bamboo tree's ability to *bounce* back or return to its original position, the word "*resilience*" comes to mind. When used in *reference* to a person this word means the ability to readily recover from shock, depression or any other situation that *stretches* the limits of a person's emotions.

Have you ever felt like you are about to snap? Have you ever felt like you are at your breaking point? Thankfully, you have survived the experience to live to talk about it.

During the experience you probably felt a mix of emotions that threatened your health. You felt emotionally drained, mentally exhausted and you most likely endured unpleasant physical

---

有感于竹子伸屈自如的能力，脑海中不由自主地闪现"韧性"这个词。当用这个词来形容人时，它表示可以很快地从打击、绝望以及其他挑战人的情感极限的状况中恢复过来的能力。

你是否有过快撑不下去的感觉？你是否曾经面临行将崩溃的边缘？感谢上苍，现在你已战胜了那段苦难，能活着回顾它。

在那段经历中，你也许觉得有一种复杂的情绪影响着你的健康。你觉得精力消耗殆尽，精疲力竭，而且还要忍受一些身体上非常不适的症状。

---

bounce *v.* 弹回；（使）弹起；弹跳
reference *n.* 提到；谈及

resilience *n.* 快速恢复的能力
stretch *v.* 伸展；拉紧

symptoms.

Life is a mixture of good times and bad times, happy moments and unhappy moments. The next time you are experiencing one of those bad times or unhappy moments that take you close to your breaking point, bend, but don't break. Try your best not to let the situation get the best of you.

A measure of hope will take you through the unpleasant *ordeal*. With hope for a better tomorrow or a better situation, things may not be as bad as they seem to be. The unpleasant ordeal may be easier to deal with if the end result is worth having.

If the going gets tough and you are at your breaking point, show resilience. Like the bamboo tree, bend, but don't break!

生活总是喜忧参半，有欢乐也有悲伤，所以下次当你又要面对那些近乎崩溃的磨难和痛苦时，可以弯弯你的腰，却不可以将它折断，尽最大的努力不要被磨难击败。

一点希望可以让我们挺过悲伤的苦难。如果拥有对美好明天的渴望，事情也许就不像现在看起来那么糟。如果最终的结局值得拥有，那么痛苦的历程也许就能轻松地过去了。

如果这路途太过辛苦，你几乎无法承受，那就展现你的韧性吧！就像那翠竹，可以弯曲，但不会被折断！

---

ordeal *n.* 严峻的考验；苦难的经历

8

A Handful of Clay

— Henry Van Dyke

There was a handful of *clay* in the bank of a river. It was only common clay, *coarse* and heavy; but it had high thoughts of its own value, and wonderful dreams of the great place which it was to fill in the world when the time came for its *virtues* to be discovered.

Overhead, in the spring sunshine, the trees *whispered* together of the glory

---

一土一大道
—— [美]亨利·范戴克

从前在河边上有这么一撮黏土。说来也不过是最普通的黏土，且质地粗糙，但它将自己的价值想象得很高，认为自己在世界上可能占有重要的地位，认为一旦时运到来，自己的美德终将为人发现。

在头顶上这明媚的春光里，树木正交头接耳地窃窃私语，纤细的林花

---

clay　*n.* 黏土；泥土
virtue　*n.* 美德；优点

coarse　*adj.* 粗的；粗糙的
whisper　*v.* 低声说；耳语；低语

which descended upon them when the delicate blossoms and leaves began to expand, and the forest glowed with fair, clear colours, as if the dust of thousands of rubies and *emeralds* were hanging, in soft clouds, above the earth.

The flowers, surprised with the joy of beauty, bent their heads to one another, as the wind *caressed* them, and said: "Sisters, how lovely you have become. You make the day bright."

The river, glad of new strength and *rejoicing* in the unison of all its waters, *murmured* to the shores in music, telling of its release from icy fetters, its swift flight from the snow-clad mountains, and the mighty work to which it was hurrying—the wheels of many mills to be turned, and great ships to be floated to the sea.

Waiting blindly in its bed, the clay comforted itself with lofty

---

和树叶开始吐放，林中一片清亮艳丽，这一切交相辉映。那情景，宛如朵朵红绿宝石所形成的彩云，轻柔地悬浮在树林上空。

花儿看到这美景惊喜极了，它们探着头，在春风中互相祝贺："姐妹们，你们出落得多可爱啊，你们真是给白日增辉。"

河水因为增添了新的力量而格外兴奋，它沉浸在水流重聚的欢乐之中，不断地以美好的音调向岸边喃喃絮语，倾诉着是怎么挣脱冰雪的束缚，怎么从积雪覆盖的群山一路跑到这里，还有它要抓紧时间去担任重大工作——无数水车轮等着它去推动，巨大的船只等着它去送往海上。

这撮黏土懵懵懂懂地待在河床，不断地用种种远大理想来安慰自己。

---

emerald n. 绿宝石；艳绿色

rejoice v. （使）欣喜;（使）高兴

caress v. 爱抚；拥抱

murmur v. 小声说

hopes. "My time will come," it said. "I was not made to be hidden forever. Glory and beauty and honour are coming to me in due season."

One day the clay felt itself taken from the place where it had waited so long. A flat *blade* of iron passed beneath it, and lifted it, and *tossed* it into a cart with other lumps of clay, and it was carried far away, as it seemed, over a rough and stony road. But it was not afraid, nor discouraged, for it said to itself: "This is necessary. The path to glory is always *rugged*. Now I am on my way to play a great part in the world."

"我的时运会到的，"它说，"我注定不会被长久地埋没的。世间的种种光辉和荣耀会在适当的时候，降临到我的头上。"

忽然有一天，黏土发现它自己被挪了位置，不在原来长期苦守的地方了。一把铁铲插在它下面，把它挖了起来，然后和别的泥土一起被装到车上，驶过一条起伏的石路，运到遥远的地方去。但是它并不害怕，也不灰心，它在心里对自己说："这是必要的。通往光荣的路总是充满艰难曲折的。现在我就要去完成我的重大使命。"

---

blade *n.* 刃；锋
rugged *adj.* 崎岖的；凹凸不平的

toss *v.* （轻轻或漫不经心地）扔；抛；掷

But the hard journey was nothing, compared with the *tribulation* and distress that came after it. The clay was put into a trough and mixed and beaten and stirred and *trampled*. It seemed almost unbearable. But there was *consolation* in the thought that something very fine and noble was certainly coming out of all this trouble. The clay felt sure that, if it could only wait long enough, a wonderful reward was in store for it...

　　但是这段辛苦的路程与它后来所经受的种种折磨痛苦相比却又不算什么。黏土被抛进一个槽子里，然后经过一番搅拌、捶打、践踏。真是苦不堪言啊！但是一想到某种美好的事物必将从这番痛苦中锤炼出来，黏土也就释然了。它坚信，只要能耐心地等待下去，总有一天会得到重酬⋯⋯

---

tribulation *n.* 苦难；艰难　　　　　　　　　　trample *v.* 踩；踏
consolation *n.* 安慰；慰问

October Lake

— *Herbert Ernest Bates*

The October leaves have fallen on the lake. On bright, calm days they lie in thousands on the now darkening water, mostly yellow *flotillas* of *poplar*, floating continuously down from great trees that themselves shake in the windless air with the sound of falling water, but on rainy days or after rain they seem to swim or be driven away, and

湖光秋色

—— [美]赫伯特·欧内斯特·贝慈

十月,树叶飘落在湖面上。在这平静晴朗的日子里,无数叶子此时落在了色泽渐渐转暗的湖面上。这些落叶大多是枯黄的白杨叶,从伟岸的杨树上纷纷凋落,在无风的空气中伴随着雨水瑟瑟发抖。但是在雨天或雨后,树叶会顺水漂走或冲走,使得湖面上一片冷清,只剩橄榄黄的睡莲残叶还漂浮在湖上。盛夏时节,这些翠绿的睡莲曾经如祖母绿

---

flotilla *n.* 小舰队;小型船队   poplar *n.* 杨树

nothing remains to break the surface except the last of the olive-yellow lily pads that in high summer covered every inch of water like emerald *porcelain*. The lilies have gone too, the yellow small-headed kind that in bud are like swimming snakes and the great *reeds* are going, woven by wind and frost into untidy basket islands under which *coot* and *moorhen* skid for cover at the sound of strangers.

All summer in this world of water lilies, the coot and moorhen lived a bewildered life. There was no place where they could swim and all day they could be seen walking daintily heads slightly aside and slightly down, across the lily-hidden water, as bemused by the world of leaves as they had been in winter by the world of ice. In the clearer water they are more active.

The lake is long and unbroken except for two small islands. The

---

的瓷器一般布满了整个湖面。但是此刻，那些曾经黄色的小花蕾，犹如水中游动的小蛇儿，此时也不复存在。大片的芦苇也凋谢了，被风霜编织成许多凌乱的篓筐似的小洲。当陌生人的声音传来时，这小洲就成了黑鸭与雷鸟的避风港。

　　整个夏季，这满是睡莲的世界里，黑鸭与雷鸟过着困惑迷茫的日子。它们找不到可以尽情戏水的地方，因此人们整天都看见它们穿梭在这片被睡莲覆盖的湖面之间，时而歪歪头，时而垂下脑袋，小心翼翼地缓缓前行，无所适从，仿佛它们置身于冬日里的冰雪世界。但若在开阔的水域里，它们就活跃得多了。

　　湖面开阔，除两处小岛外，大体连成了一片。湖上的鸟儿，仿佛被注

---

porcelain *n.* 瓷；瓷器　　　　　　　reed *n.* 芦苇；茅草
coot *n.* 黑鸭；笨蛋　　　　　　　　moorhen *n.* 〈英〉雌苏格兰雷鸟

birds, as the fit takes them, dash madly up and down it, taking off and touching down it, taking off and touching down like small fussy black sea-planes. Besides them the arrival of the wild duck, at much higher speed, is almost *majestic*. They plane down; the necks of the *drakes* shining like royal green *satin*, with the air of *squadrons* coming in after long flights from home.

It was not until late summer that fishing was possible. The water was so low and clear after drought that fish could be seen in great dark shoals, sunning themselves, shy, impossible to catch. Only in the evening, as the air cooled and the water darkened, and the surface was broken with the silver dances of the rising shoals, would you perhaps get a bite or two, a baby perch sucking at the worm, a

---

入了兴奋剂，快乐地上下翻跳，犹如一群忙碌的黑色水上小飞机。在它们旁边，飞来一群野鸭，速度极快，甚为壮观。公鸭脖子上的羽毛闪着光泽，犹如皇室深绿缎面一般的色彩，那气势仿佛是一列皇家中队从漫长的飞行中归来。

　　直到晚夏，垂钓才会成为可能。久旱过后的湖水是如此得清凉，可以看见开阔的浅滩上的鱼群在羞怯地晒着太阳，却难以捉到。只有在傍晚，当天凉了，湖水也变暗了一些，平静的湖面被大群的鱼儿打碎，你才可能逮上一两条正在吃虫的鲈鱼或是沙丁鱼大小的拟鲤。

---

majestic *adj.* 雄伟的；威严的
satin *n.* 缎；缎子

drake *n.* 公鸭
squadron *n.* 中队

roach no bigger than a sardine.

All the time, on bright hot mornings especially great *pike* would lie out in the middle of the lake in shoals of ten or even twenty, like black *torpedoes* transfixed, never moving except in sudden immense rises that raked the water-surface with rings.

It is curious, but all the life on and about water seems to belong to water. Except for a solitary *wren fidgeting* delicately about the bands under the alder trees or a robin singing in the October afternoons across the water from the islands, all the bird life is that of waterbirds. Rooks never seem to come here, nor starlings, an occasional pigeon flaps across to the woods; even the seagulls belong to the ploughed land. But wild swans come back to nest in the piles of fawn-coloured reeds in the spring...

在明媚的清晨，梭鱼经常出现在湖的中心，十条或是二十条一群，就像黑色的鱼雷水面导弹，一动不动，偶尔从湖面底下猛地出头，掀起一阵涟漪。

说来奇怪，所有水上或者水周边的生物仿佛生来就属于这片水域。除了 偶尔在赤杨树下焦躁不安的鹪鹩，或是十月午后从岛上横掠湖面引吭高歌 的知更鸟以外，这里所有的禽类都是海鸟。乌鸦从不来访，燕八哥也未曾 出现，偶尔有一只鸽子飞过树林，甚至连海鸥都飞进了耕种的土地。但当春天到来的时候，野天鹅便会回来在那浅褐色的芦苇中筑巢。

pike *n.* 梭鱼   torpedo *n.* 鱼雷；水雷
wren *n.* 鹪鹩   fidget *v.* 坐立不安；烦躁

Gone with the Wind

— *Margaret Mitchell*

The sun was now below the horizon and the red glow at the *rim* of the world faded into pink. The sky above turned slowly from *azure* to the *delicate* blue-green of a *robin*'s egg, and the unearthly stillness of rural twilight came stealthily down about her. Shadowy dimness crept over the countryside. The red furrows and the gashed red road lost

---

飘

—— [美]玛格丽特·米歇尔

落日在地平面消失了，漫天的彩霞变成了淡淡的绯红。天空渐渐由浅蓝变为知更鸟蛋般淡淡的青绿，田园薄暮中那超尘绝俗的宁静也悄悄在她周围降落。朦胧夜色把村庄笼罩起来了。晚霞照耀下猩红的土垄沟和那条仿佛刚被截开的大路，也失掉了神奇的血色而变成平凡的褐色土地了。路那边的牧园里，马儿、骡子还有奶牛静静地站在那里，从栅栏外探出头去，等待着被赶进马厩，享用晚餐。它们好像不怎么喜欢这

---

rim *n.* （圆形物体的）边；缘

delicate *adj.* 微妙的；精美的；雅致的

azure *n.* 天蓝色

robin *n.* 知更鸟

their magical blood colour and became plain brown earth. Across the road, in the pasture, the horses, mules and cows stood quietly with heads over the split-rail fence, waiting to be driven to the stables and supper. They did not like the dark shade of the thickets *hedging* the pasture creek, and they twitched their ears at Scarlett as if appreciative of human companionship.

In the strange half-light, the tall pines of the river swamp, so warmly green in the sunshine, were black against the *pastel* sky, an *impenetrable* row of black giants hiding the slow yellow water at their feet. On the hill across the river, the tall white chimneys of the Wilkes' home faded gradually into the darkness of the thick *oaks* surrounding them, and only far-off pinpoints of supper lamps showed that a house was here. The warm damp balminess of spring encompassed her sweetly with the moist smells of new-ploughed earth and all the fresh green things pushing up to the air.

树丛间黑暗的阴影，于是抽动着双耳望着斯嘉丽，期许着她的同情与怜悯。

在这奇异的半亮半暗中，河滩上高大的针叶树，原本在阳光中闪着温暖的绿色，此刻也幽暗无比，仿佛是一排无法穿越的黑色巨人，守护着脚下优哉的黄色流水。在河对面的山顶上，威尔克斯家高大的白色烟囱逐渐与周围的橡树融在了夜色中。只有远处的点点灯火还在提示着那里住着人家。春天温暖而潮湿的泥土芬芳包裹着她，空气中满是新鲜的绿的气息……

---

hedge *v.* 回避；避免
impenetrable *adj.* 不能通过的；不能穿过的

pastel *adj.* （色彩）淡的；柔和的
oak *n.* 橡树

Clouds

— *Alan Harris*

I've opened the curtain of my east window here above the computer, and I sit now in a holy theater before a sky-blue stage. A little cloud above the neighbor's trees resembles Jimmy Durante's nose for a while, then becomes *amorphous* as it slips on north. Other clouds follow, big and little and tiny on their march toward whereness. *Wisps*

浮云朵朵
—— [美]艾伦·哈里斯

我拉开了东窗电脑上方的窗帘，瞬间感觉自己仿佛置身于一个神圣的剧场，天蓝的舞台展现在面前。有好一会儿，邻居家树上飘着的那朵云真像杰米杜兰特大鼻子形状。但渐渐地，云朵向北飘移，大鼻子也就散了状。周围的云，大的、小的、丁点儿的，也随之不见了踪影。缕缕白云或前行，或散去，这是最自然不过的了。

---

amorphous *adj.* 无固定形状的　　　　wisp *n.* （烟、蒸汽的）一缕

of them lead or droop because there must always be leading and drooping.

The trees seem to laugh at the clouds while yet reaching for them with *swaying* branches. Trees must think that they are real, rooted, somebody, and that perhaps the clouds are only tickled water which sometimes blocks their sun. But trees are clouds, too, of green leaves-clouds that only move a little. Trees grow and change and *dissipate* like their *airborne* cousins.

And what am I but a cloud of thoughts and feelings and aspirations? Don't I put out tentative mists here and there? Don't I occasionally appear to other people as a ridiculous shape of thoughts without my intending to? Don't I drift toward the north when I feel the breezes of love and the warmth of compassion?

If clouds are beings, and beings are clouds, are we not all well

---

树梢随风摇曳，既像是攀附云朵，又像是在笑话他们。树肯定在想自己才是实实在在、稳扎稳打的重量级人物，而云朵只不过是积聚的水珠，只会偶尔挡住太阳的光辉。但是其实树也是一种云，一种用绿叶做的云，只不过不怎么动罢了。树也会成长、变化和消逝，与天空的浮云别无二样。

那我呢？我不也是有着思想与感情的一朵云吗？我不也是到处游走，冬风破揣测一个又一个迷雾吗？我的那些偶尔的异想天开不也常常在不经意时在人面前汇成了一团奇形怪状的云吗？在感受到爱的微风和同情的温暖时，我不也像一朵游走向北的浮云吗？

若浮云如人，人亦如浮云，我们难道不也是感受着风的力量、随风飘

---

sway *v.* （使）摇摆；（使）摇动　　　dissipate *v.* （使）消散；消失；驱散
airborne *adj.* 在空中的

advised to drift, to feel the wind tucking us in here and plucking us out there? Are we such rock-hard bodily *lumps* as we imagine?

Drift, let me. Sing to the sky, will I. One in many, are we. Let us breathe the breeze and find *therein* our roots in the spirit.

I close the curtain now, feeling broader, fresher. The act is over. *Applause* is sweeping through the trees.

流的吗？一时停留这里，一时又流转而去？难道我们就真的如自己想象的那样坚如磐石吗？

让我飘吧！我要昂首高歌。我们只是人海里的匆匆一粟，就让我们一起呼吸着微风，在其中找寻我们精神的根。

我合上窗帘，感到心胸更加开阔，头脑更加清楚。帷幕降下树丛间掌声雷动。

---

lump *n.* 团；块   therein *adv.* 在那方面；在那时；在其中

applause *n.* 热烈鼓掌；喝彩

12

The Lesson of a Tree

— Walter Whitman

I should not take either the biggest or the most picturesque tree to illustrate it. Here is one of my favorites now before me, a fine yellow poplar, quite straight, perhaps 90 feet high, and four thick at the butt. How strong, vital, enduring! How dumbly *eloquent*! What suggestions of *imperturbability* and being, as against the human *trait* of mere

树道声声
—— ［美］沃尔特·惠特曼

我不会选择最大或最特别的那棵树来描绘。因为面前有一棵我最爱的树，一棵秀丽的黄杨，笔直挺拔，树长约90英尺，根部直径则有4英尺。它瑰丽强壮，生机盎然，默然屹立，却又树道声声，谁说黄杨只能成为人们视而不见的一桩乔木？它尽显树的艺术特质与英勇自若。它是如此纯真，然而又是如此粗犷。同时，它又是默默无语，用自己的平和有力地对抗着狂风暴雨、电闪雷鸣，还有人类这样一群一遇到风

---

eloquent *adj.* 雄辩的；流利的
trait *n.* 人的个性；特征

imperturbability *n.* 沉着；冷静；无动于衷

seeming. Then the qualities, almost emotional, palpably artistic, heroic, of a tree; so innocent and harmless, yet so savage. It is, yet says nothing. How it *rebukes* by its tough and *equable serenity* all weathers, this gusty-temper'd little *whiffet*, man, that runs indoors at a mite of rain or snow. Science (or rather half-way science) scoffs at reminiscence of dryad and hamadryad, and of trees speaking. But, if they don't, they do as well as most speaking, writing, poetry, sermons—or rather they do a great deal better. I should say indeed that those old dryad-reminiscences are quite as true as any, and profounder than most reminiscences we get. ("Cut this out", as the quack mediciners say, and keep by you.) Go and sit in a grove or woods, with one or more of those voiceless companions, and read

吹草动就缩进屋子的没用的东西。科学（或是说是半吊子科学）对有关树精、树仙或者开口说话的树嗤之以鼻。但是，即便是树木不会说话，也依然同话语、写作、诗歌还有布道一样具有深意，甚至有过之无不及。我要说的是那些古老的联想也是真真切切的，甚至比大多数的联想都要深刻（"得了，别信它！"庸医这样告诉你，你也就信了。）请到林中空地坐一坐吧，与那些无言的树为伴，然后读一读前面的话，仔细想想。

rebuke *v.* 责难或指责　　　　　　　　equable *adj.* 宁静的；温和的
serenity *n.* 安详；宁静　　　　　　　whiffet *n.* 无关紧要的人；轻轻一吹

the foregoing, and think.

One lesson from *affiliating* a tree—perhaps the greatest moral lesson anyhow from earth, rocks, animals, is that same lesson of *inherency*, of what is, without the least regard to what the looker on (the critic) supposes or says, or whether he likes or dislikes. What worse—what more general malady *pervades* each and all of us, our literature, education, attitude toward each other (even toward ourselves), than a morbid trouble about seems (generally temporarily seems too), and no trouble at all, or hardly any, about the sane, slow-growing, *perennial*, real parts of character, books, friendship, marriage—humanity's invisible foundations and hold-together?

我们从树身上得到的启示，也可以说是从大地、岩石以及动物身上得到的最大启示，就是事物的内在本质与旁观者（或批评者）的揣测和评说，抑或是与他们的喜好无关。而我们中间普遍存在的糟糕问题是，人们对文学、教育等表面现象喋喋不休，而对于那些存在于人格、书籍、友谊、婚姻等连接人类的无形本质中的合理的真实视而不见。难道还有比这更糟糕的吗？

affiliate *v.* 使隶属于；使紧密联系
pervade *v.* 遍及；弥漫

inherency *n.* 固有；天赋
perennial *adj.* 长久的；持续的；反复出现的

13

Spell of the Rising Moon

—Peter Steinhart

Moon rise is slow and *serried* with *subtleties*. To watch it, we must slip into an older, more patient sense of time. To watch the moon move *inexorably* higher is to find an unusual stillness within ourselves. Our imaginations become a ware of the vast distance of space, the immensity of the earth and the huge improbability of our own existence.

月挂星空
—— ［美］皮特·斯坦哈特

月亮升得很慢，但每时每刻都有微妙的差异。为了赏月，我们需换以一种更加古老沉稳的时间感。看着月亮不可阻逆地高升，也就是在我们内心求索一份不寻常的宁静。我们会联想到宇宙的辽远、大地的广袤以及自身的渺小。我们自叹卑微却又受宠若惊。

---

serried *adj.* 密集的；靠紧的
inexorably *adv.* 无情地；冷酷地

subtlety *n.* 细微；精细；巧妙

We feel small but privileged.

Moonlight shows us none of life's harder edges. Hillsides seem silken and silvery, the oceans still and blue in its light. In moonlight we become less calculating, more drawn to our feelings.

And odd things happen in such moments. On that July night, I watched the moon for an hour or two, and then got back into the car, turned the key in the *ignition* and heard the engine start, just as mysteriously as it had stalled a few hours earlier. I drove down from the mountains with the moon on my shoulder and peace in my heart.

I return often to the rising moon. I am drawn especially when events crowd ease and *clarity* of vision into a small corner of my life. This happens often in the fall. Then I go to my hill and *await* the

---

　　月光里，生活中的坚硬棱角被抚平。山坡像丝绸般光滑，且泛着闪闪银光，大海在月光中显得格外宁静、蔚蓝。月光下的我们，少了些许算计和心机，却多了几分对情感的专注。

　　就在这时，发生了一件奇怪的事儿。在七月的一个晚上，我赏了一两个小时的月亮，然后回到车中，插进钥匙准备点火，竟然听到发动机响了起来，而就在几个小时前它自己也曾突然无故熄火。伴着空中的明月和心中的那份平静，我开车下了山。

　　后来我便经常在这里观赏月出，尤其是在被一系列琐事逼入生活的死角，而失去那份悠然和清明的时候。这经常发生在秋天。我爬上山顶，等待月亮慢慢地升起，只见在地平线上，它像巨大的金黄色的圆盘，驱走了

---

ignition　*n.*　（汽油引擎的）发火装置

await　*v.*　等候

clarity　*n.*　清楚；明晰；清澈

hunter's moon, enormous and gold over the horizon, filling the night with vision.

An owl *swoops* from the ridgetop, noiseless but bright as flame. A cricket shrills in the grass. I think of poets and musicians. Of Beethoven's "Moonlight Sonata" and of Shakespeare, whose Lorenzo declaims in The Merchant of Venice, "How sweet the moonlight sleeps upon this bank! / Here will we sit and let the sounds of music / Creep in our ears." I wonder if their verse and music, like the music of crickets, are in some way voices of the moon. With such thoughts, my *citified* confusions melt into the quiet of the night.

Lovers and poets find deeper meaning at night. We are all apt to

---

黑暗，带来了光明。

　　一只猫头鹰从山顶俯冲而下，悄无声息，犹如焰火一样明亮。一只蟋蟀在草丛中高声鸣叫。这令我想起了诗人与音乐家，想起了贝多芬的《月光奏鸣曲》和莎士比亚的《威尼斯商人》中洛伦佐的话："月光在这河岸边睡得多么甜蜜！/ 我们坐下，让音乐之声 / 悄然潜入我们的耳朵。"我不知道他们那优美的诗歌与玄妙的音乐，是否像蟋蟀的歌声一样，是某种意义上的月亮的低吟呢。想着这些，我对城市的迷惑全都融化在这宁静的夜里。

　　恋人以及诗人们在夜里能领略到更深刻的生活意义。而我们则更容易

---

swoop　*v.*　俯冲；猛冲　　　　　　　citified　*adj.*　都市风的；有都市气概的

pose deeper questions—about our origins and destinies. We *indulge* in riddles, rather than in the impersonal *geometries* that govern the daylit world. We become philosophers and mystics.

At moonrise, as we slow our minds to the pace of the heavens, *enchantment* steals over us. We open the *vents* of feeling and exercise parts of our minds that reason locks away by day. We hear, across the distances, murmurs of ancient hunters and see anew the visions of poets and lovers of long ago.

提出更深层的问题——我们的起源和命运的归属。比起毫无人情味却支配着日常生活的几何学，这个迷更容易使我们沉醉。我们都成了哲学家与神秘主义者。

月亮升起，我们放慢自己的思绪，以跟随天堂的脚步，一种痴迷遍布全身。我们会打开情感的大门，让白天被理智锁住的思绪尽情舞蹈。我们穿越时空，听见远古猎人的喃喃细语，看到古时诗人与恋人们眼中的世界。

---

indulge *v.* 使（自己）沉溺于   geometry *n.* 几何（学）
enchantment *n.* 魅力；迷人之处   vent *n.* 宣泄（情感）

Time for Sunshine

— Anonymous

Having spring around makes you feel different after such a long winter journey. How well do you feel when you have a little bit of sunshine in your life? What effect does it do have on our *psyche*? The power of sunshine brings us a lot of comfort, *optimism*, self-confidence and of course a smile. Imagine how great it would be if we were so positive all year round!

光影下的光阴
—— 佚名

漫长的冬季过后，春天带给人不同的感觉。当生活中有些许阳光时，你感觉有多好？阳光对我们的精神到底有着什么影响？阳光使我们获得安慰、乐观与自信，当然还有微笑。想象一下，如果一年到头我们都有这么积极的心态，那该多好！

---

psyche *n.* 灵魂；心灵　　　　optimism *n.* 乐观；乐观主义

Living like this is possible if you really think about it. In order to exist in such a state of happiness though, we must have sunshine *radiating* from within ourselves, shining from our hearts, our minds and from our souls. I bet many of you are reading this now and saying "Yeah that is easier said than done!" And what do we say to that well, in the end that's your choice and if you think that way then your own life will *reflect* that attitude of yours!

In order to make "sunshine" or rather, "light" a part of our being. It is so important that you watch your thoughts, your words and your actions so that you do not *contradict* what you really feel you'd like to create in your own life. Watch your thoughts and really become aware of how many *negative* thoughts pass through your mind about yourself and other people around you. Watch to see how often you gossip about other people and when you become aware of it you will see how often it is actually attached with feelings of jealousy, envy

---

倘若你真想的话，像这样生活也是可能的。然而为了以这样快乐的状态生活，我们就必须让自己的心灵、头脑和灵魂都充满阳光。我相信很多正在阅读此篇文章的人都会说："是啊，说着容易，做起来难！"对此该说些什么呢？最后作决定的是你自己。你的想法将会反映出你的生活态度！

为了使"阳光"，抑或"光明"内化成为我们生命的一部分，重要的一点就是：我们得去审视自己的思想，言语和行为，确保自己的意愿不和生命中的创造相矛盾。注意审视自己的思想，特别是注意那些闪现在脑海里的对自己和周围人的消极看法。注意检查自己是否经常说别人的闲话，当你意识到这些时，就会明白这些做法实际上源于嫉妒、羡慕以及不安感。

---

radiate *v.* 发射出（光、热等）
contradict *v.* 与……发生矛盾

reflect *v.* 反照；映出
negative *adj.* 消极的；负面的

and insecurity about yourself.

You should also take a close look at your "intention". How many of you do something for another person without expecting to receive something in return? It might not even have to be a material or physical thing you expect, expecting *recognition* or acknowledgement for what you have done is enough to create conditions on your intention. Think about it! We may not always pay attention to what our true intentions are behind our words, thoughts and actions because many of us are not aware of the power and effect they have when it comes to creating our lives.

Putting all of what I have said together, it seems that most of

我们都应该好好审视自己的"动机"。我们当中有多少人在为别人做事时却从不求回报？你期待的回报不一定非得是物质上的或身体上的，期待认可或感谢已经足以成为动机了。思考一下！我们可能不会总是注意自己的思想和言行背后的真正动机，那是因为我们中的许多人并没有意识到光影下的光阴动机对生活的影响力。

综合以上我所说的，似乎我们中的大多数人都在内心中制造出了一个怪物。我们只是在讨论、思考，而在帮助别人的时候并没有带着赤诚的真心。所有这些都源于一种"否定"的态度。当谈到给生活带来更明亮的

recognition *n.* 承认；认可

us are creating *monsters* inside of us just by simply talking, thinking and not putting our heart out with the right *intention* towards helping someone else. All of these things are born from a "negative" attitude and will not help us in any way at all when it comes to bringing a brighter "sunshine" into our lives. If you took all your negative attitudes in one hand and measured your need to feel "sunshine" in the other, you would see how both these elements really contradict each other.

Be brave and break your patterns and your habits this spring and by doing so you will allow the true sunshine to take place by radiating out from your heart and into your life and the lives of the people who are around you!

"阳光"时，它根本不会对我们有所帮助。假如你把所有的消极态度都放在一只手中，并在另一只手上衡量你对"阳光"的需要，你就会发觉，这些因素彼此有多么抵触。

请勇敢些吧！在这个春天里，打破你以往的固有模式和习惯，这样你将让真正的阳光照耀自己，这阳光发自内心，照耀你的生活，也照耀着周围人的生活！

---

monster *n.* 怪物　　　　　　　　　intention *n.* 意图；目的

Thunderstorm

— *Mark Twain*

There was a *brooding* oppressiveness in the air that seemed to *bode* something. Presently there came a quivering glow that vaguely revealed the *foliage* for a moment and then vanished. By and by another came, a little stronger. Then another. There was a pause. Now a *weird* flash turned night into day and

雷雨滂沱
—— [美]马克·吐温

空气中浮动着令人憋闷的压抑，仿佛要把一切都包围。不一会儿，远处划过一道闪光，隐约照在树叶上，只一闪便又消失了。不久，又划过一道更为强烈的闪光。接着又是一道。之后便是一阵沉寂。这时，一道更为奇异的闪电将暗夜照耀得如同白昼。可以清楚地看见

---

brooding *adj.* 郁闷的
foliage *n.* 植物的叶子（总称）

bode *v.* 预示；预告；预言
weird *adj.* 怪诞的；超然的

showed every little grass blade, separate and distinct. A deep peal of thunder went rolling and tumbling down the heavens and lost itself in *sullen rumblings* in the distance. A sweep of chilly air passed by, rustling all the leaves and snowing the *flaky* ashes broadcast about the fire. Another fierce glare lit up the forest and an instant crash followed. A few big rain drops fell pattering upon the leaves.

A *furious* blast roared through the trees, making everything sing as it went. One blinding flash after another came, and peal on peal of deafening thunder. And now a drenching rain poured down and the rising hurricane drove it in sheets along the ground. Now the battle

---

每一棵小草的叶子，一片片，清晰得很。一阵沉雷轰轰隆隆当空滚过，渐去渐远，消失在遥远的天边。一阵凉风袭来，树叶沙沙作响，火堆里的灰，雪花似地四处飞散。又一道闪电点亮了森林，响雷紧随其后。几颗硕大的雨点噼里啪啦地砸在叶子上。

　　一阵狂风吹过树梢，整个林子都唱响了起来。一道道令人眩晕的闪电接踵滑落，一阵阵震耳的雷鸣紧随而至。现在，倾盆大雨劈头泼下。上升的飓风将雨滴洒满大地，这场战斗达到了高潮。在这无休止的燃着道道闪电的天空下，透过雨帘，我瞥见万事万物都露出了清晰的面目与线条：被

---

sullen *adj.* （天空或天气）阴沉的

flaky *adj.* 成片的；薄而易剥落的

rumbling *n.* 隆隆声；辘辘声

furious *adj.* 狂怒的；暴怒的

was at its highest. Under the ceaseless conflagration of lightning that flamed in the skies, everything below stood out in clean-cut and shadowless *distinctness*: the bending trees, the *billowy* river, white with foam, the driving spray of spume flakes, the dim outlines of the high bluffs on the other side, glimpsed through the drifting cloud rack and the *slanting* veil of rain. Every little while some giant tree yield the fight and fell crashing through the younger growth; and the unflagging thunderpeals came now in earsplitting *explosive* bursts, keen and sharp, and unspeakably appalling.

风吹弯的树木，白浪飞腾的大河，大片随风飞舞的泡沫以及河对岸高耸的悬崖峭壁的模糊轮廓，都在那飞渡的乱云和斜飘的雨幕中乍隐乍现。每隔一会儿，都有一棵大树不敌狂风，哗啦一声倒在小树丛中。而电闪雷鸣仍在源源不断地继续着，尖锐锋利，犹如爆炸的力量，夹杂着难以言说的恐怖。

distinctness *n.* 不同；明显　　　　billowy *adj.* 大浪的；巨浪似的
slaning *adj.* 斜的；不直的；歪的　　explosive *adj.* 爆炸的；爆发的；易爆炸的

16

Spring

— James J. Kilpatrick

Springs are not always the same. In some years, April bursts upon Virginia hills in one *prodigious* leap and all the stage is filled at once, whole *choruses* of *tulips*, arabesques of *forsythia*, cadenzas of flowering plum. The trees grow leaves overnight.

In other years, spring tiptoes in. It pauses, overcome by shyness, like my

---

春暖人间
—— [美]詹姆斯·基尔帕特里克

春不总是千篇一律的。有时候，四月仿佛一下子就跃上了弗吉尼亚的山头。顿时，整个舞台都活跃起来了。郁金香在引吭高歌，大片的连翘花在翩翩起舞，梅花在表演独奏。树木也在一夜之间披上了新绿。

有时，春天又悄然来临。她欲前又止，羞涩腼腆。像我的孙女一样在门口窥探一下又跑开，笑声在走廊中回荡。"我知道你在那儿！"我喊，

---

prodigious *adj.* 异常的；惊人的
tulip *n.* 郁金香

chorus *n.* 合唱；合唱队
forsythia *n.* 连翘属植物

grandchild at the door, peeping in, ducking out of sight, giggling in the hallway. "I know you're out there," I cry. "Come in!" And April slips into our arms.

The *dogwood* bud, pale green, is inlaid with *russet* markings. Within the perfect cup a score of *clustered* seeds are nestled. One examines the bud in awe: where were those seeds a month ago? The apples display their milliner's scraps of *ivory* silk, rose-tinged. All the sleeping things wake up—primrose, baby iris, blue phlox. The earth warms—you can smell it, feel it, crumble April in your hands.

Look to the rue anemone, if you will, or the pea patch, or to the stubborn weed that thrusts its shoulders through a city street. This is how it was, is now, and ever shall be, the world without end. In the serene certainty of spring recurring, who can fear the distant fall?

"进来呀！"于是四月便倏地一下飞进我们的怀抱。

浅绿色的茱萸花镶在褐色的花边上。完美的花儿中零落着点点种子。我们不禁要惊羡地问一句："一个月前这些种子还在哪儿呢？"苹果树则像是镶着玫瑰红的象牙缎帽。所有曾经沉睡的都已经清醒：报春花、小鸢尾还有蓝色的夹竹桃。大地回暖了，你可以闻到四月的气息，感觉到它那股馨香，把它捧在手中赏玩。

如果你愿意，看看芸香海葵，或者是豌豆畦，抑或是城市街道的缝隙间那倔强的野草。它们从前是这样，现在是这样，将来还会是这样，这是 个永不停息的世界。在恬静之中，春去春回，还有谁会害怕那遥远的秋天呢？

---

dogwood *n.* 山茱萸   russet *adj.* 黄褐色的

clustered *adj.* 丛生的；群集的   ivory *n.* 象牙质；象牙色；乳白色

17

The Enchantment of Creeks

— Peter Steinhart

Nearly everybody has a creek in his past, a *confiding* waterway that rose in the spring of youth. A park *ranger*'s voice softens as he talks of a boyhood creek in Louisiana where he swam and fished. A conservationist's eyes *sparkle* as he recalls building dams on Strawberry Creel in the California of his youth. An Ohio woman feels suddenly at home again as

魅力溪流
—— [美]皮特·斯坦哈特

几乎每个人的过去都流淌着一条小溪，它发源于人生的春日——少年时代，一路潺潺向前。一位守林人每每谈起他孩提时在故乡路易斯安那游泳、钓鱼的小溪时，语气便立刻温柔起来。一位环保员回忆他年轻时在加利福尼亚草莓溪筑水坝的经历时，眼中闪着奇异的光芒。而一位来自俄亥俄州的妇女一想起在她父母屋后的小溪里捉小虾的情景，顿时感到重新回到了故乡。

---

confiding *adj.* 相信人的；易于相信的　　　　　　ranger *n.* 护林者
sparkle *v.* 闪闪发光；闪耀

she remembers catching crayfish in the creek behind her parent's house.

My creek wound between Grandfather's *apricot* orchard and a neighbor's hillside pasture. Its banks were shaded by *cottonwoods* and redwood trees and a thick tangle of *blackberries* and wild grapevines. On hot summer days the quiet water flowed clear and cold over gravel bars where I fished for trout.

Nothing historic ever happens in these recollected creeks. But their persistence in memory suggests that creeks are bigger than they seem, more a part of our hearts and minds than mighty rivers.

Creek time is measured in the lives of strange creatures in sand-flecked caddis worms under the rocks, sudden gossamer clouds of mayflies in the afternoon, or minnows darting like slivers of inspiration into the dimness of creek fate. Mysteries float in creeks'

　　我心中的那条小溪位于祖父的杏树园和邻居的半山的草地间。小溪被三叶杨和红杉遮得严严实实，岸边长满了黑莓和野葡萄。烈日炎炎的夏季，清澈透凉的溪水静静地流过满是砾石的沙滩，我就在那儿钓鳟鱼。

　　在这些记忆中的小溪里从没有发生过什么惊天动地的大事，但是它们却深深扎根在脑海之中，挥之不去。这也说明它们比看上去要博大得多，已然成了我们记忆的一部分。在这一点上，那些激流澎湃的大河就无法相比了。

　　那些有关小溪的时光可以用奇妙的小生物来衡量：那些躲藏在岩石底下的沙斑石蚕；或者午后时分一闪而过如浮云的蜉蝣；抑或在水中窜来窜去，闪着灵光的那些米诺鱼。小溪的神奇漂荡在涟漪间，蔓生在卵石密布

---

apricot　*n.* 杏子；杏树　　　　　　　cottonwood　*n.* 三叶杨；棉白杨
blackberry　*n.* 黑莓

riffles, crawl over their *pebbled* bottoms and slink under the roots of trees.

While rivers are heavy with sophistication and sediment, creeks are clear, innocent, *boisterous*, full of dreams and promise. A child can wade across them without a parent's *cautions*. You can go it alone, jig for crayfish, swing from ropes along the bank. Creeks belong to childhood, drawing you into the wider world, teaching you the curve of the earth.

Above all, a creek offers the mind a chance to *penetrate* the alien universe of water, of tadpoles and trouts. What drifts in creek water is the possibility of other worlds inside and above our own. Poet Robert Frost wrote: "It flows between us, over us, and with us. And it is time, strength, tone, light, life, and love."

的水底，隐藏在树根之下。

如果说大河深不可测，那么小溪则清澈、纯洁、欢乐，充满梦想与期望。无须父母的告诫，孩子就可以趟过小溪。他们可以独自去小溪里捉小虾，还可以在岸边系上绳子荡秋千。小溪属于童年，将孩子们带到更加广阔的世界，让他们领略到大地的跌宕起伏。

最重要的是，小溪为心灵提供了一个深入到属于蝌蚪和鳟鱼的水世界的机会。溪水中流走的是一个别样的世界，它既存在于我们的世界之中，又凌驾在这个世界之上。诗人罗伯特·弗罗斯特曾经写道："小溪潺潺流淌着，在我们之中，在我们之上，跟我们融为一体。小溪是时间、力量、乐曲、光明、生命和爱。"

---

pebbled *adj.* 多卵石的
caution *n.* 小心；谨慎；慎重

boisterous *adj.* 喧闹的；狂欢的
penetrate *v.* 看透；深入于

18

Flowery Tuscany

— D.H.Lawrence

North of the Alps, the *everlasting* winter is *interrupted* by summers that struggle and soon yield; south of the Alps, the everlasting summer is interrupted by *spasmodic* and *spiteful* winters that never get a real hold, but that are mean and dogged. The inbetween, in either case, is just as it may be. But the lands of the sun are south of the Alps, forever.

花花视界
—— [英]劳伦斯

夏季奋力要打断阿尔卑斯山北部漫长的冬天，但很快就退却。而在南麓，漫漫长夏也被令人厌恶的冬季陆续骚扰。寒风顽固肆虐，却始终占不了上风。两种情况迥然不同，但有一点是肯定的，太阳永远照耀在山的南边。

---

everlasting *adj.* 永久的；持续延长的
spasmodic *adj.* 一阵阵的

interrupt *v.* 打扰；打断
spiteful *adj.* 故意使人苦恼的

In the morning, the sun shines strong on the horizontal green cloud-puffs of the pines, the sky is clear and full of life, the water runs *hastily*, still browned by the last juice of crushed olives. And there the earth's bowl of *crocuses* is amazing. You cannot believe that the flowers are really still. They are open with such delight, and their *pistil* thrust is so red-orange, and they are so many, all reaching out wide and marvellous, that is suggests a perfect *ecstacy* of radiant, throughing movement, lit-up violet and orange, and surging in some invisible rhythm of concerted, delightful movement. You cannot believe they do not move, and make some sort of crystalline sound of delight. If you sit still and watch, you begin to move with them, like moving with the stars, and you feel the sound of their radiance. All the little cells of the flowers must be leaping with flowery life and

---

清晨，当耀眼的阳光辉映着绿云般的松树，天空万里无云，生机勃勃。湍急的流水依旧被橄榄树残枝染成了深棕色。看，那一簇簇的藏红花开得正艳。你都无法相信这些花是静止不动的。花儿绽放，花蕊橙红，热情洋溢，光芒四射，使人心醉神迷。花潮涌动，五光十色，伴着隐隐约约和谐欢乐的节奏摇摆。你一定能感觉花的灵动，发出清脆的欢乐之歌。如果坐下来观赏，你也会不由自主地随着它们轻轻摇摆，就像跟随着星星的脚步，耳边仿佛听到那欢乐的旋律。花儿身上所有的细胞都轻舞着，诉说着花语。

---

hastily *adv.* 匆忙地；仓促地   crocus *n.* 番红花属；番红花
pistil *n.* 雌蕊   ecstacy *n.* 狂喜；出神；入迷

utterance.

And now that it is March, there is a rush of flowers. Down by the other stream, which turns sideways to the sun, and tangles by the *brier* and *bramble*, down where the *hellebore* has stood so wan and *dignified* all winter, there are now white tufts of primroses, suddenly come. Among the tangle and near the water-lip, tufts and bunches of primroses, in abundance. Yet they look more wan, more pallid, more flimsy than English primroses. They lack some of the full wonder of the northern flowers. One tends to overlook them, to turn to the great, solemn-faced purple violets that rear up from the bank, and above all, to the wonderful little towers of grape hyacinth.

This is the time, in March, when the sloe is white and misty in the hedge-tangle by the stream, and on the slope of land the peach tree

---

  时值三月，百花竞放。在另一条奔向太阳的小溪的旁边，在纷乱的野蔷薇与荆棘中间，在虽憔悴却保有尊严而站立了一冬的藜芦下面，大片的报春花开了。在沙洲上，水岸边，大片大片的报春花妖娆着，但是看上去却比英国的报春花还要苍白、脆弱、了无生气。它们似乎缺少北麓花儿的那种生的力量。人们常常对它们视而不见，而把目光投向岸边表情庄重的紫罗兰，还有那一串串洋水仙构成的小花塔。

  三月的这个时候，溪边的树丛中黑刺李的花如烟如雾，坡上粉色的桃花树亭亭玉立。浅粉色的杏花儿纷纷落下。可是深色的桃花依旧盛放着，

---

brier   *n.* 荆棘；野蔷薇   bramble   *n.* 荆棘

hellebore   *n.* 菟葵；藜芦   dignify   *v.* 使显得威严；使高贵；使显赫

stands pink and alone. The almond blossom, silvery pink, is passing, but the peach, deep-toned, bluey, not at all *ethereal*, this reveals itself like flesh, and the trees are like isolated individuals, the peach and the *apricot*.

It is so conspicuous and so individual, that pink among the coming green of spring, because the first flowers that emerge from winter seem always white or yellow or purple. Now the celandines are out, and along the edges of the pond, the big, *sturdy*, black-purple anemones, with black hearts...

有血有肉丝毫没有去意。树木就像是独立的个体，桃树如此，杏树亦如此。

春天的新绿中夹杂着粉红，是那么夺目，那么独特。因为冬天褪去，首先开的花儿应该是白色、黄色或是紫色。白屈菜也长出来了，而池塘的边沿，生长着高大结实的黑紫色的银莲花，带着黑色的花蕊……

---

ethereal *adj.* 轻飘的；缥缈的
sturdy *adj.* 结实的；强壮的

apricot *n.* 杏；杏仁；杏树

Snow Season

— Anonymous

The early snows fall soft and white and seem to heal the *landscape*. There are as yet no tracks through the drifts, no muddied *slush* in the roads. The wind sweeps snow into the scars of our harvest-time haste, smoothing the brow of hill, hiding *furrow* and *cog* and trash in

---

雪 之 美
—— 佚名

轻盈、洁白的雪花，纷纷扬扬地飘落，似乎在抚慰大地。积雪上还没有留下任何足迹，道路上也没有踏脏的雪泥。风夹杂着雪花覆盖了人们丰收后的大地。它抚平了山脊，藏匿了庭院内的车辙和轮齿，让杂物无影无踪。大雪还令那金属摩擦的刺耳声和机器运转时的嘈

---

landscape *n.* 风景；景色
furrow *n.* 车辙；犁沟

slush *n.* 雪泥；半融雪
cog *n.* 齿轮

the yard. Snow muffles the shriek of metal and the rasp of motion. It covers our flintier purposes and brings a redeeming silence, as if a curtain has fallen on the strivings of a year, and now we may stop, look *inward*, and *rediscover* the amber warmth of family and conversation.

At such times, locked away inside wall and woolen, *lulled* by the *sedatives* of wood-smoke and candlelight, we recall the competing claims of nature. We see the branch and bark of trees, rather than the sugar-scented green of their leaves. We look out the window and admire the elegance of ice crystal, the bravely patient tree leaning leafless into the wind, the dramatic shadows of the stooping sun. We look at the structure of things, the geometry of branch and

---

杂声变得柔和起来。它在埋没了我们的坚韧决心的同时，又赋予了一种静谧，宛如一年的努力就此落下帷幕，告一段落。现在我们也许应该驻足，审视内心，重新感受亲人团聚的温馨。

在这样的时节里，紧闭房门，裹上毛衣，沉浸在木材燃烧的温暖与烛光带来的祥和之中，我们禁不住回想起大自然的悖论。眼里看到的是枝杈和树皮，而不是散着甜香的绿叶；望向窗外，我们惊叹着，冰晶的美不胜收，钦佩光秃秃的树枝始终勇敢地迎风而立，赞美落日的身影楚楚动人；

---

inward *adj.* 内在的；内心的
lull *v.* 使安静；平静

rediscover *v.* 再次（重新）发现
sedative *n.* 镇静药；镇静剂；能使安静的东西

snowflake, family and deed.

Even before the first snow, winter has started to make us see the world differently. We watch the lawn settle into the sleep of frost and the last leaf shake on the oak, and feel the change. At night the skies are cold and clear, and stars shine like the dreams of *serpents*. The hillsides turn brown and gray. Dark clouds settle on the mountain ridges. Then comes the snow. When snowflake drifts the road, we head indoors and resign ourselves to the quiet *crackle* of the wood fire. The example of the woodpile and the well-stocked *larder* tells us that we can achieve what we dream, and winter brings us long, silent nights to dream on.

我们观察着事物的结构、树枝与雪花的形状，还有家庭事业。

其实在第一场雪到来之前，冬天就已经让我们用不同的方式看待这个世界了。我们看见：草坪早已习惯地沉睡在冰霜的包裹下，最后一片橡树叶在枝头颤抖，好像体会到了季节的变化。晚空凛冽晴朗，繁星闪烁，就像魔鬼的幻梦。山坡被染成了棕灰色，乌云爬上山脊。接着，下雪了。当片片雪花在路面堆积的时候，我们回到屋内，让自己沉醉在炉火轻微的噼啪声中。成堆的柴草和贮存好的食物表明我们可以美美地睡上一觉了。而冬日带来了宁静的漫漫长夜，正好入梦。

---

serpent *n.* 阴险毒辣的人；魔鬼　　　　　crackle *n.* 噼啪声；爆裂声
larder *n.* 食物贮藏室；食品柜

Walking to the Seacoast

— Rachel. Carson

One of my own favorite *approaches* to a rocky seacoast is by a rough path through an evergreen forest that has its own *peculiar enchantment*. It is usually an early morning tide that takes me along that forest path, so that the light is still pale and fog drifts in from the sea beyond. It is almost a ghost forest, for among the living spruce and balsam are many dead

海 之 滨
—— [美] 雷切·尔卡森

穿过一片常青林，就到了岩石遍布的海边。这是我最爱的一条通向海滨的凹凸小路，它有着自己独特的魅力。通常是清晨的潮汐吸引 我走上这林中的小径。那时，天色灰白，远处的海面浮起层层薄雾。这个时候的林子，仿佛鬼魅，因为在活生生的云杉和香脂树间，混杂着许多早已枯萎的树木。这些枯萎的树木有的依然挺立，而有的则倒在地

approach *n.* 接近；走近；靠近　　　　peculiar *adj.* 奇怪的；特有的
enchantment *n.* 魅力；迷人之处

trees—some still erect, some sagging earthward, some lying on the floor of the forest. All the trees, the living and the dead, are clothed with green and silver *crusts* of *lichens*. *Tufts* of the bearded lichen or old man's beard hang from the branches like bits of sea mist tangled there. Green woodland mosses and a yielding carpet of *reindeer* moss cover the ground. In the quiet of that place even the voice of the surf is reduced to a whispered echo and the sounds of the forests are but the ghosts of sound—the faint sighing of evergreen needles in the moving air; the creaks and heavier groans of half-fallen trees resting against their neighbors and rubbing bark against bark; the light rattling fall of a dead branch broken under the feet of

---

上。所有这些树，不论生死，都披着一层绿色和银色的地衣。一簇簇须毛丛生的地衣犹如老人的胡须从树枝上挂下，就像海平面上的一缕缕薄雾。绿色的林地苔藓和一层不断蔓延的驯鹿苔藓覆盖着地面。置身于这片宁静之地，海浪的声音几乎减弱为喃喃细语，而森林之声也宛如声之幽灵，那是四季常青的松针在风中微微叹息，还有那半折腰的树撞击着相邻树干发出的摩擦声，更有那因松鼠踩过而折断的枯树枝掉落在地后反复弹动，发出轻微的嘎嘎声。

---

crust n. （泥土、雪等）硬的外层　　　　lichen n. 地衣
tuft n. （头发、羽毛、草等）一簇；一束　　reindeer n. 驯鹿

WALKING TO THE SEACOAST

a squirrel and sent bounding and ricocheting earthward.

But finally the path emerges from the dimness of the deeper forest and comes to a place where the sound of surf rises above the forest sounds—the hollow boom of the sea, rhythmic and insistent, striking against the rocks, falling away, rising again.

Up and down the coast the line of the forest is drawn sharp and clean on the edge of a seascape of surf and sky and rocks. The softness of the sea fog blurs the *contours* of the rocks; gray water and gray mists merge offshore in a dim and *vaporous* world that might be a world of creation, stirring with new life.

　　但是，沿着幽深丛林的小径，我来到了一个海浪声盖住森林声的地方。这里，我能听得到海低沉的轰鸣声，它有节奏地拍打着礁石，落下去，又升起来，反反复复。

　　岸边的树林轮廓分明，加上海浪、天空和岩石，仿佛是一幅海景画。海面上的雾模糊了岩石的形状，远处灰暗的海水与雾气勾画出一个幽暗深邃的世界。在那世界里，仿佛会有汹涌的暗潮，创造出新的生命来。

---

contour *n.* 外形；轮廓　　　　　　vaporous *adj.* 蒸气多的；模糊不清的

Late Summer

—— *Ernest Hemingway*

In the late summer of that year we lived in a village that looked across the river and the plain to the mountains. In the bed of the river there were *pebbles* and *boulders*, dry and white in the sun, and the water was clear and swiftly moving and blue in the channels.

Troops went by the house and down the road and the dust they raised

---

夏也迟暮
—— [美]欧内斯特·海明威

那年晚夏，我们住在了一个村子里。隔着河流与平原可以望见远山。河床上布满了鹅卵石与砾石，在阳光的照耀下显得又干又白。河水很清，蓝蓝的在河道中轻快地流淌。

军队沿着乡间路走过排排房屋的时候，总会扬起一阵尘埃，这尘埃就落在了树叶上。不止如此，树干也变得灰突突的。那年树叶早落，我们看

---

pebble *n.* 鹅卵石；小圆石   boulder *n.* 巨石；巨砾

powdered the leaves of the trees. The trunks of the trees too were dusty and the leaves fell early that year and we saw the troops marching along the road and the dust rising and leaves, stirred by the breeze, falling and the soldiers marching and afterward the road bare and white except for the leaves.

The plain was rich with crops; there were many *orchards* of fruit trees and beyond the plain the mountains were brown and bare. There was fighting in the mountains and at night we could see the *flashes* from the *artillery*. In the dark it was like summer lightning, but the nights were cool and there was not the feeling of a storm coming.

Sometimes in the dark we heard the troops marching under the window and guns going past pulled by *motor-tractors*. There was

---

着军队在路上行进，尘土飞扬。而叶子，随着风，飘摇而下。士兵们踏过的路上只剩下哗哗的落叶，一眼望去白晃晃、空荡荡的。

平原上有丰饶的庄稼；有成片的果园，在平原的另一边则是褐色的光秃的群山。山中在打着仗，我们常常在夜里看见炮火的光亮，黑暗之中，竟有几分像夏夜里的闪电。只是夜里阴凉，可没有夏天风雨欲来前的那种闷热。

有的时候，黑暗之中，我们能够听见军队从窗下走过的声响，还有机动牵引机拖着大炮经过的响声。夜里交通繁忙。路上有许多驮着弹药的

---

orchard *n.* （通常指围起来的）果园

artillery *n.* 炮；大炮

flash *n.* 闪光；闪光物

motor-tractor *n.* 机动拖拉机；机动牵引机

much traffic at night and many *mules* on the roads with boxes of *ammunition* on each side of their *packsaddles* and gray motor-trucks that carried men, and other trucks with loads covered with *canvas* that moved slower in the traffic. There were big guns too that pass in the day down by tractors, the long barrels of the guns covered with green branches and green leafy branches and vines laid over the tractors. To the north we could look across a valley and see a forest of chestnut trees and behind it another mountain on this side of the river. There was fighting for that mountain too, but it was not successful, and in the fall when the rains came the leaves all fell from

骡子，运送士兵的灰色卡车，还有一种卡车，装的东西用帆布盖着，缓慢地行进着。白天，也会有卡车载着大枪大炮。一桶桶的枪支上面盖着树枝，绿色的带着浓密叶子的藤枝覆盖着整个卡车。如果向北看，在一条峡谷的后面，可以隐约见得一片板栗树林。在那树林后面，河的一边，还有着另一群远山。那群山间也打着仗，但是进展得不顺利。秋天来了，秋雨降临。树的叶子也一片片地落下，树枝于是又变得光秃秃的，雨水冲刷的

mule *n.* 骡子   ammunition *n.* 弹药；军火
packsaddle *n.* 驮鞍   canvas *n.* 帆布

the chestnut trees and the branches were bare and the trunks black with rain. They *vineyards* were thin and bare-branches too and all the country wet and brown and dead with the autumn. There were mists over the river and clouds on the mountain and trucks *splashed* mud on the road and the troops were muddy and wet in their capes; their *rifles* were wet and under their capes the two leather cartridge-boxes on the front of belts, gray leather boxes heavy with the packs of clips of thin, long 6.5 mm, *cartridges*, bulged forward under the capes so that the men, passing on the road, marched as though they were six months gone with child.

树干呈现出了灰褐色。葡萄架的藤蔓消瘦了下去，也是光秃秃的。乡间的一切潮湿、灰暗，与这秋天一起了无生气。河上升起了薄雾，山间有了乌云，卡车过去，道路上满是稀泥，连带着士兵的身上都是。身上的来复枪湿了，前胸上挂着两排皮制的子弹套，灰色的套夹里装满了细长的6.5毫米子弹，向前突着，以至于这些正在行进的士兵们一个个看起来像怀了六个月的身孕。

---

vineyard *n.* 葡萄园
rifle *n.* 步枪；来复枪

splash *v.* 使（液体）溅起
cartridge *n.* 子弹；弹药筒；弹壳

22

April Showers Bring May Flowers

— *Josh*

From the golden-tipped fields of mid-west America to the ancient kingdoms of *verdant* Palestine, there is a happy truth to be shared with all who would take *heed*. In more recent times, this truth has been expressed as: April showers bring May flowers. This is a truth that promises light bursting from darkness, strength born from weakness and, if one

雨洒花开
—— [美] 乔希

从美国中西部金色的田野，到巴勒斯坦翠绿色的古老平原，那些留心观察的人共享着同一个快乐的真理。现在这条真理被表达为：四月雨浇灌出五月花。这是一条宣告光明从黑暗之中走来的真理，它预示着坚强生于软弱，而如果你敢于相信，那生的力量就会从死亡

verdant *adj.* （草、田地等）翠绿的；嫩绿的　　　　　heed *n.* 留心；注意

dares to believe, life emerging from death.

Farmers all over the world know the importance and *immutability* of the seasons. They know that there is a season to plant and a season to harvest; everything must be done in its own time. Although the rain pours down with the *utmost relentlessness*, ceasing all outdoor activities, the man of the field lifts his face to the heavens and smiles. Despite the inconvenience, he knows that the rain provides the *nourishment* his crops need to grow and flourish. The torrential rains in the month of April, give rise to the glorious flowers in the month of May.

But this ancient truth applies to more than the crops of the fields; it is an invaluable message of hope to all who experience tragedy in life. A dashed relationship with one can open up the door to a

之中迸发。

　　全世界的农民都知道季节的重要性与不变性。他们知道什么季节播种，什么季节收获。每件事都必须应时而做。虽然暴雨无情地倾盆而下，迫使户外劳作停止，但田地的主人却会仰天微笑。尽管大雨会带来诸多不便，但他知道，雨水会为他的庄稼带来繁茂生长所必需的营养。四月的豪雨会浇灌出五月的繁花。

　　但是这一古老的真理并不仅仅适用于庄稼。对于那些正经历着人生磨难的人们来说，这真理会带给他们无限的希冀：一段友谊的受挫会开启另一段崭新友谊的大门；这厢失去的工作说不定正为那厢更好的工作提供

immutability *n.* 永恒性；不变性　　　　utmost *adj.* 极度的；最大的
relentlessness *n.* 残酷；无情　　　　　nourishment *n.* 食物；滋养品

brand new friendship with another. A lost job here can provide the opportunity for a better job there. A broken dream can become the foundation of a wonderful future. Everything has its place.

Remember this: *overwhelming* darkness may *endure* for a night, but it will never overcome the *radiant* light of the morning. When you are in a season of *sorrow*, hang in there, because a season of joy may be just around the corner...

了机会；一个破碎的梦会成为美好前程的基石。万事万物都有其存在的道理。

请记住吧：势不可挡的黑暗只不过持续一个夜晚，它永远无法遮挡清晨的万丈光芒。因此，当你陷入悲伤之时，请坚持住，因为欢乐的季节也许就在转角处……

---

overwhelming *adj.* 势不可挡的；压倒一切的　endure *v.* 持续；持久；坚持下去
radiant *adj.* 放热的；发光的；光芒四射的　　sorrow *n.* 悲痛；悲伤；遗憾；懊悔

Dawn Watch

—— John Ciardi

There is an old mountain *laurel* on the island of the driveway *turnaround*. From somewhere on the wind a white morning- glory rooted next to it and has climbed it. Now the laurel is woven full of white bells tinged pink by the first rays through the not quite mist. Only in earliest morning can they be seen. Come out two hours from now and there will be no

守候黎明
—— [美]约翰·西尔迪

在回旋车道的岛上，有一颗古老的月桂树。旁边的某个迎风处还长着一株白色的牵牛花，扎根月桂旁，并且攀缘其上。此刻，月桂树上布满的白色喇叭花在清晨的薄雾与阳光中变成了粉色。然而此景只有在清晨才能看到。此后两个小时，牵牛花将不复盛开。

laurel *n.* 月桂树   turnaround *n.* 车辆调头处

morning-glories.

Dawn, too, is the hour of a weed I know only as day flower—a bright blue button that closes in full sunlight. I have weeded *bales* of it out of my flower beds, its one daytime virtue being the *shallowness* of its root system that allows it to be pulled out effortlessly in great handfuls. Yet, now it shines. Had it a few more hours of such shining in its cycle, I would *cultivate* it as a ground cover, but dawn is its one hour, and a garden is for whole days.

There is another blue morning weed whose name I do not know. This one grows from a bulb to *pulpy* stems and a bedraggled daytime sprawl. Only a shovel will dig it out. Try weeding it by hand and the stems will break off to be replaced by new ones and to sprawl over the chosen plants in the flower bed. Yet, now and for another hour it

---

黎明也是鸭拓草的天下，这是一种白日里闭合的亮蓝色小花。我在自己的花坛里已经拔走了好几拨。因为它的生长期短、根基浅，所以极易被大把大把地拔除。黎明是属于它的美好时光。它盛开着、闪耀着。倘若它可多开几个小时，我会考虑将其栽成地被。然而黎明是它的唯一时光，而花园是为长长的白昼设计的。

还有一种我不知道名字的蓝色草。它从球茎开始长出多汁的叶子，蔓延在地面，只有用铲子才能清除。如果尝试用手去拔，茎就会折断，从而长出新茎，再生长覆盖住其他的植物。然而此刻与接下来的一个小时，也是属于它的时刻。它的花虽然只有鸭拓草的四分之一大，颜色也比其他白

---

bale *n.* 包；捆
cultivate *v.* 耕；种植

shallowness *n.* 浅；表面
pulpy *adj.* 果肉状的；多汁的

outshines its betters, its flowers about the size of a quarter and paler than those of the day flower but somehow more brilliant, perhaps because of the contrast of its paler *foliage*.

And now the sun is slanting in full. It is bright enough to make the leaves of the Japanese red maple seem a *transparent* red *bronze* when the tree is between me and the light. There must be others, but this is the only tree I know whose leaves let the sun through in this way—except, that is, when the fall colors start. Aspen leaves, when they first yellow and before they dry, are transparent in this way. I tell myself it must have something to do with the red-yellow range of the *spectrum*. Green takes sunlight and holds it, but red and yellow let it through...

日里开放的花要苍白许多，但是不知怎的，这花就是显得更加明艳，或许是暗淡的叶子衬托的关系。

现在，太阳开始发挥它的全部威力了。要是日本红枫叶夹在我与光线之间，看上去就是透明的红青铜色。其他的树肯定还有，但是日本枫树却是我唯一知道的可以让阳光有这种效果的树。除非当秋季降临，白杨叶开始泛黄但还没干枯之前，也会产生这种效果。我告诉自己，这一定与光谱中的红、黄光波有关。绿光挡住并吸收了太阳的光线，而红色与黄色则允许阳光的穿越……

---

foliage *n.* 植物的叶子（总称）
bronze *n.* 青铜色；赤褐色

transparent *adj.* 透明的；清澈的
spectrum *n.* 光谱

The Song of the River

— *W.S. Maugham*

You hear it all along the river. You hear it, loud and strong, from the *rowers* as they urge the *junk* with its high *stern*, the mast lashed alongside, down the swift running stream. You hear it from the trackers, a more breathless *chant*, as they pull desperately against the current, half a dozen of them perhaps if they are taking up wupan, a couple of hundred if they are

大河之歌
—— [美] W. S. 毛姆

沿河上下都可听得见那歌声。你听，它响亮有力，那是船夫的号子，他们划着木船顺流而下，船尾高高翘起，桅杆系在船舷。你听，这还有更急促的号子，那是纤夫。他们拉纤逆流而上。如果拉的是小木船，也许就只五六个人；如果拉的是扬着帆的大船过险滩，那就得要二百多人。船中央有一个汉子在那击鼓助威，为他们鼓劲。于是纤夫

---

rower *n.* 划船者；划手
stern *n.* 船尾；艉

junk *n.* 舢板
chant *n.* 单调的歌；单调的语调

hauling a splendid junk, its square sail set, over a rapid. On the junk, a man stands *amidships* beating a drum *incessantly* to guide their efforts, and they pull with all their strength, like men possessed, bent double; and sometimes in the *extremity* of their *travail* they craw on the ground, on all fours, like the beasts of the field. They strain, strain fiercely, against the pitiless might of the stream. The leader goes up and down the line and when he sees one who is not putting all his will into the task he brings down his split bamboo on the naked back. Each one must do his utmost or the labour of all is vain. And still they sing a vehement, eager chant, the chant of the turbulent waters. I do not know words can describe what there is in it of effort. It serves to express the straining heart, the breaking muscles, and at the same time the indomitable spirit of man which overcomes the pitiless force of nature. Though the rope may part and the great junk swing back, in the end the rapid will be passed; and at the close of

---

们使出全部力量，犹如神灵附体，腰弯成两折，用力向前。有时候，力量用到极限，就会全身趴在地上匍匐前进，像田里的牲畜。他们使劲，拼命使劲，对抗着无情的流水。领头的在纤绳前后跑来跑去，如果看到有人没有全力以赴，就拿起竹板，打在他光着的背上。每个人都必须竭尽所能，否则就会功亏一篑。然而即便是这样，他们还是喊着激昂而热烈的号子，那和着澎湃河水的号子。我不知道用怎样的词语才能描绘其中所包含的拼搏。号子表现的是紧绷的心弦，几乎要断裂的筋肉，同时，也有人类誓与无情的自然抗争的顽强精神。绳可断，船可退，但最终必将通过险滩。一

---

amidships *adv.* 在船中部；向船的中部
extremity *n.* 末端；尽头

incessantly *adv.* 不断地；不停地
travail *n.* 辛苦

the weary day there is the hearty meal...

But the most *agonizing* song is the song of the coolies who bring the great bales from the junk up the steep steps to the town wall. Up and down they go, endlessly, and endless as their toil rises their rhythmic cry. He, aw—ah, oh. They are *barefoot* and naked to the waist. The sweat pours down their faces and their song is a groan of pain. It is a sigh of despair. It is heart-rending. It is hardly human. It is the cry of souls in infinite distress, only just musical, and that last note is the ultimate sob of humanity. Life is too hard, too cruel, and this is the final despairing protest. That is the song of the river.

天结束，纵然筋疲力尽，但还可以痛痛快快地吃上一顿饱饭……

然而最叫人难受的却是苦力的歌。他们背着船上卸下的硕大的包裹，沿着陡坡爬上堤坝。他们不停地上上下下，随着无尽的劳动响起有节奏的喊声：嗨，呦——嗬，噢。他们赤着脚，光着背，汗水肆无忌惮地从脸上流下。那号子是痛苦的呻吟，绝望的叹息，震慑人心，简直不是人的声音。那是灵魂在无尽悲戚中加上了音乐节奏的呐喊。那最后一声是人类最凄苦的抽泣。生活太过艰难、太过残酷，而这呐喊正是最终绝望的抗议。这呐喊就是那大河之歌。

---

agonizing *adj.* 使人痛苦的；痛苦难忍的 　　　　　barefoot *adj.* 赤脚的

25

Go into the Wilderness

── *Ralpha Waldo Emerson*

To go into *solitude*, a man needs to retire as much from his *chamber* as from society. I am not solitary whilst I read and write, though nobody is with me. But if a man would be alone, let him look at the stars. The rays that come from those heavenly worlds, will separate between him and *vulgar* things...

To speak truly, few adult persons can

旷野之寂

── ［美］拉尔夫·沃尔多·爱默生

为了到达孤独的境界，人就应该像离开社会一样离开卧室。读书写作的时候，虽然并没有人陪着我，但是我并不孤独。然而一个人若是想要独处，就请他看看星星吧。那些来自天国的光芒会把他和世俗之事分隔开来……

老实说，没有几个成年人能看穿自然。大多数人没看清太阳，至少，

---

solitude *n.* 独处；独居　　　　　　　　chamber *n.* 卧室；寝室；私人房间
vulgar *adj.* 庸俗的；粗俗的；低级的

see nature. Most persons do not see the sun. At least they have a very superficial seeing. The sun *illuminates* only the eye of the man, but shines into the eye and the heart of the child. The lover of nature is he whose inward and outuard senses are still truly adjusted to each other; who has retained the spirit of infancy even into the era of manhood. His *intercourse* with heaven and earth, becomes part of his daily food. In the presence of nature, a wild delight runs through the man, in spite of real sorrows.

In the woods too, a man casts off his years, as the snake his *slough*, and at what period *soever* of life, is always a child.

There I feel that nothing can befall me in life—no disgrace,

他们所见只是浮光掠影。阳光只照亮了成年人的双眼所见，但却能照进孩童的眼睛与心灵深处。只有自然的真正热爱者才能做到外部感觉和内心感觉的和谐，尚能在成年时保有婴孩的心灵。与天地的交流成了他每日食材的一部分。在自然面前，纵然有哀伤，但是兴奋仍旧贯穿了他整个身心。

在林中，人们抖落岁月如同蛇蜕掉旧皮，无论身处生命的哪一阶段，都会心如孩童。

在这里，我不会感到任何痛苦的压迫——没有耻辱，没有不幸，而且这些缺憾是自然所无法修复的。站在空地上，小我的一切都消失了，我似

---

illuminate *v.* 使明亮；照亮
slough *n.* 蜕下的皮（或壳）

intercourse *n.* 往来；交往；交际
soever *adv.* 无论；不论何种

no calamity, which nature cannot repair. Standing on the bare ground—all mean *egotism* vanishes. I become a transparent eyeball. I am nothing. I see all. The currents of Universal Being *circulate* through me; I am part or particle of God. The name of the nearest friend sounds then foreign and accidental. To be brothers, to be acquaintances—master or servant, is then a trifle and disturbance. I am the lover of uncontained and immortal beauty. In the wildness, I find something more dear and *connate* than in streets or villages. In the *tranquil* landscape, and especially in the distant line of the horizon, man beholds somewhat as beautiful as his own nature.

乎化作一个透明的眼球，无形无影，但却能看到一切。我不复存在；我洞察一切；宇宙之流在我周身循环；我成为上帝的一部分，我是他的粒子。这个时候，即便是最亲密的朋友的名字听起来也是陌生而无足轻重的。兄弟，朋友，主人或仆人，一切变得细碎卑微。我爱着这永恒不朽之美。在旷野里，我体味到比在街市和村庄里更可贵的东西。在这安详的风光里，尤其是在远方的地平线上，人们会看到如此美丽的大自然，美丽犹如我们自身的本性。

---

egotism *n.* 自我中心；自尊自大
connate *adj.* 天生的；先天的

circulate *v.* （使）循环；（使）流通
tranquil *adj.* 安静的；平静的；宁静的

26

Night and Moonlight

— *Henry David Thoreau*

Night is certainly more novel and less *profane* than day. I soon discovered that I was *acquainted* only with its complexion, and as for the moon, I had seen her only as it were through a *crevice* in a shutter, occasionally. Why not walk a little way in her light?

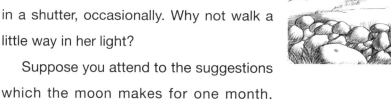

Suppose you attend to the suggestions which the moon makes for one month,

月夜清辉
—— [英]亨利·大卫·梭罗

比起白昼，黑夜当然要多一点奇异而少一点世俗。我很快就发现自己认识的仅仅是夜的表象，而至于月亮，我也仅仅偶尔从百叶窗的罅隙间瞥见而已。那为什么不出去在月光下走走呢？

假如你认真思考一下月亮徒劳无功地照耀了一个月、丝毫不起作用的论调，得到的结论是否有别于文学与宗教中有关月亮的结论呢？可为什么不学习一下眼前鲜活的案例呢？如果月亮来复又去，带着自己的诗世界与

profane *adj.* 世俗的
crevice *n.* 裂缝

acquaint *v.* 使认识；使了解

commonly in vain, will it not be very different from anything in literature or religion? But why not study this Sanscrit? What if one moon has come and gone with its world of poetry, its weird teachings, its *oracular* suggestions, so divine a creature *freighted* with hints for me, and I have not used her? One moon gone by unnoticed?

I think it was Dr. Chalmers who said, criticising Coleridge, that for his part he wanted ideas which he could see all round, and not such as he must look at away up in the heavens. Such a man, one would say, would never look at the moon, because she never turns her other side to us. The light which comes from ideas which have their orbit as distant from the earth, and which is no less cheering and enlightening to the *benighted* traveller than that of the moon and stars, is naturally reproached or *nicknamed* as moonshine by such. They are moonshine, are they? Well, then do your night-travelling

---

古怪的教条还有预言，这个神性的灵物给了我暗示，而我却没有利用呢？一轮不被注意的月亮？

我想查尔墨博士在讨论柯勒律治的时候说过，在他看来，他需要的是身边可以看见全貌的思想，而不是像月亮这样只有一面，并且还得仰起头到天国去找寻。这样的人，我们可以说，从来不屑于月亮，因为月亮不会把另一面也展现给人类。从远离地球的星球那边发射出的光芒有着自己的轨道，对夜行者来说，这样的光亮是令人欣喜而鼓舞的。可是人们常常笑话好似从月亮上发出的光一样细微又遥远的思想为月光。它们是月光，不是吗？那好吧，就让你在没有月光指引下的夜里继续你的前行好了。我很

---

oracular *adj.* 神谕的；难解的
benighted *adj.* 星夜赶路的

freight *v.* 运送；使充满
nickname *v.* 给……起绰号

when there is no moon to light you; but I will be thankful for the light that reaches me from the star of least *magnitude*. Stars are lesser or greater only as they appear to us so. I will be thankful that I see so much as one side of a celestial idea, —one side of the rainbow, —and the sunset sky.

Men talk *glibly* enough about moonshine, as if they knew its qualities very well, and *despised* them; as owls might talk of sunshine. None of your sunshine, —but this word commonly means merely something which they do not understand, —which they are abed and asleep to, however much it may be worth their while to be up and awake to it.

It must be allowed that the light of the moon, *sufficient* though it is for the pensive walker, and not disproportionate to the inner light we have, is very inferior in quality and intensity to that of the sun.

感激哪怕是微小的星星散发出的光亮。若说星星渺小或是伟大，那只是我们的感觉罢了。虽然只能看到一面，但我已经是感激不尽了，哪怕这是彩虹的一面、落日的一面。

人们滔滔不绝地谈月亮，仿佛对它所有的特质了如指掌，并且鄙视它，这就像猫头鹰探讨日光一样。人类的阳光在猫头鹰看来根本无法理解，它们在白天里入眠，对醒过来观察日光这件事根本不理不睬。

所以说，即使月光只能给深思的夜行者照路，即使是微小得连我们内心的光亮也比不上，即使与太阳相比差了许多，它也是理应存在并且合理的。

---

magnitude *n.* 星球的亮度
despise *v.* 鄙视；藐视

glibly *adv.* 流利地；随便说出口的
sufficient *adj.* 充足的；足够的

The Bounty of the Sea

—— Jacques Yves Cousteau

During the past thirty years, I have observed and studied the oceans closely, and with my own two eyes I have seen them sicken. Certain *reefs* that teemed with fish only ten years ago are now almost lifeless. The ocean bottom has been raped by *trawlers*. Priceless *wetlands* have been destroyed by land fill. And everywhere are sticky globs of oil, plastic

海纳百川

—— [法] 雅克·伊夫·库斯托

在过去的三十年中，我密切地关注与研究着海洋。我亲眼看见了他们病入膏肓。十年前鱼群环绕的礁石现已了无生气。海底仿佛被撒网的渔民强暴了一番。价值连城的湿地也被填为陆地。每到一处，都漂浮着一小团一小团黏稠的油污、塑料垃圾还有许多看不见的有毒的排放物。通常当我讨论到海洋的疾病时，都会听到这样的评述："它们只是

reef *n.* 礁；暗礁
wetland *n.* 潮湿的土壤；沼泽地

trawler *n.* 拖网渔船

refuse, and unseen clouds of poisonous effluents. Often, when I describe the symptoms of the oceans' sickness, I hear remarks like " they're only fish" or " they're only whale" or "they're only birds". But I assure you that our destinies are linked with theirs in the most profound and fundamental manner. For if the oceans should die—by which I mean, that all life in the sea would finally cease—this would signal the end not only for marine life but for all other animals and plants of this earth, including man.

With life departed, the ocean would become, in effect, one enormous *cesspool*. Billions of decaying bodies, large and small, would create such an insupportable *stench* that man would be forced to leave all the coastal regions. But far worse would follow.

The ocean acts as the earth's *buffer*. It maintains a fine balance between many salts and gases which make life possible. But dead seas would have no buffering effect. The carbon *dioxide* content of

---

鱼、鲸、禽。"但是我相信我们的命运与这些鱼和禽以最深远与最根本的方式紧密地联系在一起。如果海洋死去——我的意思是说海洋的生物停止了生命——这不仅仅意味着海洋生命的终结，也意味着地球上所有生物生命的终结，这其中也包括人类。

生物没有了生命，海洋就会变成巨大的污水池。成千上万的死尸，大的、小的，会散发出冲天的臭气，致使人类会远离海岸。但更糟的还在后面。

海洋就如同地球的减震器。它有助于维持盐与气体的平衡，以使生命能够存活下去。但是一个死亡的海洋却不能起到这种作用。大气中的二氧

---

cesspool n. 污水坑；化粪池
buffer n. 缓冲器；减震器

stench n. 臭气；恶臭
dioxide n. 二氧化物

the atmosphere would start on a steady and remorseless climb, and when it reached a certain level a " greenhouse effect" would be created. The heat that normally radiates outward from the earth to space would be blocked by the CO_2 and sea level temperatures would dramatically increase.

One *catastrophic* effect of this heat would be melting of the icecapes at both the North and South Poles. As a result, and ocean would rise by 100 feet or more, enough to flood almost all the world's major cities. These rising waters would drive one-third of the earth's billions inland, creating *famine*, fighting, *chaos*, and disease on a scale almost impossible to imagine.

Meanwhile, the surface of the ocean would have *scummed* over with a thick film of decayed matter, and would no longer be able to give water freely to the skies through evaporation. Rain would become a rarity, creating global drought and even more famine...

化碳会稳步持续攀升，当它达到一定程度，就会产生"温室效应"。地面散发出的热不能穿过二氧化碳，于是导致海平面的温度急剧上升。

这种热力带来的致命后果之一就是南北极冰川的融化。其结果就是海平面上升100英尺或者更多，到时候，许多大的城市都变成了一片汪洋。这些上涨的海水会覆盖全球三分之一数十亿计的陆地，造成几乎无法想象的大规模饥 荒、战乱、混乱以及瘟疫。

与此同时，海洋的表面会被厚厚的一层腐烂的东西覆盖，不能通过蒸发提供水汽，也就不会降雨，全球就会陷入干旱，甚至饥荒……

---

catastrophic *adj.* 灾难性的
chaos *n.* 混乱；紊乱

famine *n.* 饥荒
scum *v.* 被浮渣覆盖

28

A Green Hill Far Away

—— *John Galsworthy*

Was it indeed only last March, or in another life, that I climbed this green hill on that day of *dolour*, the Sunday after the last great German offensive began? A beautiful sun-warmed day it was, when the wild *thyme* on the southern slope smelled sweet, and the distant sea was a glitter of gold. Lying on the grass, pressing my check to its warmth, I tried

青山常在
—— [英]约翰·高尔斯华绥

是在这刚刚过去的三月里，抑或是在另一个世界里，我登上了那座青山？那是一个痛苦的日子——德国发动最后一次大进攻之后的星期天。那是一个阳光明媚的日子，南坡上的野茴香芳香扑鼻，远方的大海闪烁着一片金黄。我躺在草地上，用面颊贴着那温暖，为解除新的恐惧而寻找安慰。持续四年的战祸使这场进攻愈发显得残忍。

---

dolour *n.* 悲伤；伤心

thyme *n.* （用以调味的）百里香（草）

to get solace of that new dread which seemed so cruelly unnatural after four years of war-misery.

" If only it were all over!" I said to myself: " and I could come here, and to all the lovely places I know, without this *awful* contraction of the heart, and this knowledge that at every tick of my watch some human body is being *mangled* or destroyed. Ah, if only I could! Will there never be an end!"

And now there is an end, and I am up on this green hill once more, in December sunlight, with the distant sea a glitter of gold. And there is no cramp in my heart, no *miasma* clingling to my senses. Peace! It is still *incredible*. No more to hear with the ears of the nerves the ceaseless roll of gunfire, or see with the eyes of the nerves drowning men, gaping wounds, and death. Peace, actually peace!

"愿这一切快些结束吧！"我喃喃自语道，"那时我就又能到这里来，到一切我熟悉的可爱地方去，而不致这么伤神揪心。我的表针每滴答一下，就有一批生灵惨遭涂炭。啊，要是我有这个能力该多好！这场战事难道永远不能结束吗？"

现在总算结束了，于是我在阳光明媚的十二月，又一次登上这青山。远处的海面依旧一片金黄。但此时的我，心头不再阵痛，感官也不再被瘴气侵袭。和平了！仍然有些难以相信。再也不用紧张万分地竖起耳朵去倾听那永无休止的枪炮声，再也不用看到那些溺水的人们、撕裂的伤口与死亡。和平了，真的和平了！战争持续了如此长的时间，以至于我们不少人

---

awful *adj.* 糟糕的；可怕的；惊人的
miasma *n.* 瘴气；难闻的气体

mangle *v.* 损毁；使伤残；使变形
incredible *adj.* 不能相信的；不可信的

The war has gone on so long that many of us have forgotten the sense of *outrage* and amazement we had, those first days of August, 1914, when it all began. But I have not forgotten, nor ever shall.

In some of us—I think in many who could not voice it—the war has left chiefly this feeling: " If only I could find a country where men cared less for all that they seem to care for, where they cared more for beauty, for nature, for being kindly to each other. If only I could find that green hill far away!" Of the songs of Theocritus, of the life of St. Francis, there is no more among the nations than there is of dew on grass in an east wind. If we ever thought otherwise, we are disillusioned now. Yet there is peace again, and the souls of men fresh murdered are not flying into our lungs with every breath we

---

似乎已经忘记了1914年8月战争初期的愤怒与错愕。但是我没有忘记，我永远不会忘记。

这场战争给我们的一些人——我想还有许多人，只是他们表达不出罢了——主要留下了这种感觉：“但愿我能找到这样一个国家，在那里，人们所关心的不再是我们一向所关心的那些，他们关心的是美，是自然，是对彼此的仁爱。但愿我能找到远处的那座青山！”俄忒克里托斯的诗篇与圣弗西斯的高风，在当今的各个国家里，已无处找寻，正如那草上的露珠消失在东风里一样。即便我们过去有过不同的想法，但如今也破灭了。不过和平终究还是来了，那些新近被屠杀的人们的幽魂总归不会再随着我们呼吸而堵塞我们的肺。

---

outrage *n.* 义愤；愤慨

draw.

Each day this thought of peace becomes more real and blessed. I can lie on this green hill and praise Creation that I am alive in a world of beauty. I can go to sleep up here with the *coverlet* of sunlight warm on my body, and not wake to that old dull *misery*. I can even dream with a light heart, for my fair dreams will not be spoiled by waking, and my bad dreams will be cured the moment I open my eyes.

每天，想着和平在变得愈发真实和幸福。我已能卧在这座青山之上，为生活在这样一个美丽的世界而赞美造物主。我也能在这温暖阳光的覆盖之下安然入眠，而不会醒来重复那恹恹欲绝的滋味。我甚至能满心喜悦地去做梦，不致因为醒来而扫兴，并且即使做了噩梦，醒后一切也就一如往常。

---

coverlet *n.* 覆盖物　　　　misery *n.* 痛苦；苦恼；苦难

29

A River

— Anne Morrow Lindbergh

Our first sign of China was indicative of the immensity of the country we were going to. It was an unexpected sign, for flying over the Yellow Sea from Japan, we were looking for land on the *horizon* ahead, perhaps even the *outline* of mountains like the horizon behind us. But long before the darker blue of solid land

---

河水悠悠

——［美］安妮·默洛·林德伯格

引领我们前往中国的首要标志便是，我们即将前往的是一个地域如此广袤的国家。这标志是如此出人意料，因为从飞离日本、跨过黄海起，我们期待看到的是和被我们抛在身后的一样的陆地与山脉。但是早在深色的陆地在湛蓝的海面那边上升露头之前，中国就已然迎接了我们。我们已经能够充分看到面前的这片海与身后的那片海之间的差别。

---

horizon *n.* 地平线；范围；界限

outline *n.* 外形；轮廓；略图

began to rise above the shifting blue of the sea, China came out to meet us. We were aware of a difference in color between the water in front of us and the water behind us, a sharp line of *demarcation* when brown waves met blue. Mud from the Yangtze River darkened the sea for miles ahead. We were approaching China.

What a river this must be to make itself felt so far out from land, to so impress its personality on its *overlord*, the sea. I made *obeisance* to it in my mind, for I felt in the presence of a great monarch. And I was not mistaken. The Yangtze River, as we followed its smooth course up through the immense stretches of flat farm land of coastal China, was one of those rivers which give the impression of being the only true and permanent rulers of the earth.

Rivers perhaps are the only physical features of the world that are at their best from the air. Mountain ranges, no longer seen in

---

因为眼前看到的是截然不同的棕色与蓝色海水划界相接这样戏剧化的一幕。扬子江带来的泥沙染黑了入海口外几英里的海水。我们正一步步地向中国靠拢。

那是一条多么特殊的河流啊！甚至在离陆地很远的地方，你就可以感受到它的存在。它的个性给它的君王——大海以深刻的震慑。就连我也在心里向它屈服了，因为我觉得仿佛帝王莅临在我面前。我并没有说错。沿着它的河道深入，观赏它在中国大地一马平川上的流转，你会感到它才是这个星球上唯一真正永恒的统治者。

河流也许是世界上各种地貌中唯一从空中才能看得最清晰的地貌。从空中鸟瞰，山脉因为失去了展示其伟岸侧面的机会而沦为蚁丘；海洋失去

---

demarcation *n.* 划界；立界   overlord *n.* 最高领主；霸主

obeisance *n.* 敬礼；敬意

profile, dwarf to *anthills*; seas lose their horizons; lakes have no longer depth but look like bright pennies on the earth's surface; forests become a thin impermanent film, a moss on the top of a wet stone, easily rubbed off. But rivers, which from the ground one usually sees only in cross sections, like a small sample of ribbon rivers *stretch* out serenely ahead as far as the eye can reach. Rivers are seen in their true stature.

They rumble down mountain sides; they *meander* through flat farm lands. Valleys trail them; cities ride them; farms cling to them; road and railroad tracks run after them and they remain, permanent, possessive. Next to them, man's gleaming *cement* roads which he has built with such care look fragile as paper streamers thrown over the hills, easily blown away. Even the railroads seem only scratched in with a penknife. But rivers have carved their way over the earth's face for centuries and they will stay.

了漫长的海岸线为其增辉；湖泊失去了深邃，看起来更像是地球表面闪闪发光的硬币；而森林呢，森林变成了单薄而转瞬即逝的胶片，或变成了湿石头上的青苔，似乎很容易被擦掉，然而河流却与之相反。在地面上看时，我们通常只能见到一小段，但是自空中看去，它就像一条缎带，安详宁静地向前伸展着，一直到你看不见的尽头。它全部的容颜才得以展现。

它们冲下山脊，蜿蜒穿过平坦的农田。山谷被它们甩在后面，城镇被它们穿过，农庄紧贴着它们，公路和铁路追赶在它们后面，而河流仍然保持永恒不变的坚定气场。在它们旁边，人类精心建造的闪闪发光的水泥路看上去如同洒在山上的细纸彩带一样弱不禁风，似乎随时便会被吹走。甚至铁路也只是像用铅笔刀胡乱刻出来似的。唯独河流，数百年来，在地球的表面雕刻上自己的印记，并将继续延续下去。

---

anthill *n.* 蚁丘；人群密集的地方　　　　stretch *v.* 伸展；拉紧

meander *v.* （指溪流、河流等）蜿蜒而流　　cement *n.* 水泥

At the Edge of the Sea

— Rachel Louise Carson

The shore is an ancient world, for as long as there has been an earth and sea there has been this place of the meeting of land and water. Yet it is a world that keeps alive the sense of continuing creation and of the *relentless* drive of life.

Each time that I enter it, I gain some new awareness of its beauty and its deeper meanings, sensing that *intricate*

缤纷海岸线
—— [美] 蕾切尔·路易斯·卡逊

海岸是一个古老的世界，因为自从有地球和大海以来，就有这个水陆相接的地方。它是一个让人们感到不断创造生命、驱动生命向前的世界。

每当我踏入这个世界，都会感受到它的美与深沉的内涵，感受到生物之间错综复杂的关系：每一种生命都与其他生命紧密地链接在一起。

---

relentless *adj.* 不停的；不懈的；不间断的　　　　intricate *adj.* 错综复杂的

fabric of life by which one creature is linked with another, and each with its surroundings.

In my thoughts of the shore, one place stands apart for its *revelation* of *exquisite* beauty. It is a pool hidden within a cave that one can visit only rarely and briefly when the lowest of the year's low tides fall below it, and perhaps from that very fact it acquires some of its special beauty. Choosing such a tide, I hoped for a *glimpse* of the pool. The ebb was to fall early in the morning. I knew that if the wind held from the northwest and no interfering swell ran in from a distant storm the level of the sea should drop below the entrance to the pool. There had been sudden *ominous* showers in the night, with rain like handfuls of gravel flung on the roof. When I looked out into the early morning the sky was full of a gray dawn light but the

---

　　每当我想起海岸，最先浮现在眼前的是一个有着独特魅力的地方，那是一个隐匿于洞中的潭。一年当中只有海潮降落到最低，低于水潭时，人们才能在这难得的短时间内看见它。也许正因如此，它才平添了某种特别的美。我选好这样一个低潮的时机，希望能看一眼水潭。根据以往的情况推算，潮水将在清晨退去。我知道如果不刮西北风，如果没有远处的风暴掀起的海浪进行干扰，海平面就会落得比水潭的入口还低。夜里突然下了几场不祥的阵雨，一把把碎石般的雨点洒落在屋顶上。清晨我向外眺望，只见灰蒙蒙的曙光笼罩着天空，只是太阳还没有升起。水和空气一片暗淡。海湾对面的西天上挂着一轮明月，月下就是远方的海岸呈现出的一条

---

revelation n. 意想不到的事物；非常好的事物　　　exquisite adj. 精致的；精美的
glimpse n. 一瞥；一看　　　　　　　　　　　　　ominous adj. 不吉的；不祥的

sun had not yet risen. Water and air were pallid. Across the bay the moon was a luminous disc in the western sky, suspended above the dim line of distant shore—the full August moon, drawing the tide to the low, low levels of the *threshold* of the alien sea world. As I watched, a gull flew by, above the *spruces*. Its breast was rosy with the light of the unrisen sun. The day was, after all, to be fair.

Later, as I stood above the tide near the entrance to the pool, the promise of that rosy light was sustained. From the base of the steep wall of rock on which I stood, a moss-covered ledge jutted seaward into deep water. In the surge at the rim of the ledge the dark fronds of *oarweeds* swayed, smooth and gleaming as leather. The projecting ledge was the path to the small hidden cave and its pool. Occasionally a swell, strong than the rest, rolled smoothly over such

---

灰色的线——8月的满月导致了落潮，潮水直降到那与人世隔离的海世界的门槛。在我观望的时候，一只海鸥从云杉上面掠过，腹部被即将喷薄而出的朝阳染成了绯红。天终于放晴了。

后来，当我置身于水潭入口处时，四周已是瑰红色的晨光。从我立脚的峭岩底部，一块青苔覆盖的礁石伸向大海的最深处。礁石周围是摇摆的水藻，犹如皮面一般光滑。那些凸现的礁石即是通往隐藏的通口以及洞中水潭的路径。偶尔一阵强劲的波涛优雅地绕过礁石。这阵阵波涛的间隙足以让我踏上礁石，窥探那仙境般的水潭，那鲜为人观的水潭。

---

threshold *n.* 门口；门槛　　　　　　　　　　spruce *n.* 针枞；云杉
oarweed *n.* 昆布；叶片状海藻

swells were long enough to admit me to the ledge and long enough for a glimpse of that fairy pool, so seldom and so briefly *exposed*.

And so I knelt on the wet carpet of sea moss and looked back into the dark *cavern* that held the pool in a shallow *basin*. The floor of the cave was only a few inches below the roof, and a mirror had been created in which all that grew on the ceiling was reflected in the still water below.

于是，我就跪在那海苔铺成的湿漉漉的地毯上，向那黑洞里窥探，就是这些黑洞把水潭塑造成了浅盆的模样。只见洞的底部距离顶部仅有几英寸。水面纹丝不动，犹如一面明镜，映出了洞顶上的一切生物。

---

expose *v.* 暴露；显露；露出

basin *n.* 盆

cavern *n.* 大山洞；大洞穴

Nature

— *Ralph Waldo Emerson*

To go into solitude, a man needs to retire as much from his chamber as from society. I am not *solitary* whilst I read and write, though nobody is with me. But if a man would be alone, let him look at the stars. The *rays* that come from those heavenly worlds, will separate between him and what he touches. One might think the atmosphere was made transparent

---

论 自 然
——拉尔夫·沃尔多·爱默生

人若想体味孤独，需远离社会、走出房间。我于读写之际，虽无人做伴，但仍不觉孤独。不过一人独处时，还请仰望星空。天宇之光将独处者与身边琐事隔开。设想空气之所以设计成透明状，乃是为将天体之永恒壮景示于人间。从城市街道望去，繁星何其伟大！倘若满天

---

solitary *adj.* 独处的；孤单的　　　　　　　　　ray *n.* 光束；光线

with this design, to give man, in the heavenly bodies, the perpetual presence of the sublime. Seen in the streets of cities, how great they are! If the stars should appear one night in a thousand years, how would men believe and adore; and preserve for many generations the *remembrance* of the city of God which had been shown! But every night come out these *envoys* of beauty, and light the universe with their admonishing smile. The stars awaken a certain *reverence*, because though always present, they are inaccessible; but all natural objects make a kindred impression, when the mind is open to their influence. Nature never wears a mean appearance. Neither does the wisest man *extort* her secret, and lose his curiosity by finding out all her perfection. Nature never became a toy to a wise spirit. The flowers, the animals, the mountains, reflected the wisdom of his best

---

繁星需历经千年方能现身一夜，人类该是怎样信仰、怎样崇敬，曾示于世人的上帝之城又将保留多少代人的记忆！然而，这美丽的使者夜夜出现，带着劝解的微笑，将宇宙点亮。满天星辰尽管常在，却又遥不可及，于是便将某种敬畏之心唤醒。然而，人类若敞开心扉，自然之物便留下熟稔亲切的味道。自然从不做吝啬状。最睿智者亦无法穷尽其秘密，不会在了解其完美后丧失好奇心。自然绝不会成为智者的玩具。鲜花、动物、山峦，一如曾赋予智者无忧无虑的童年，无不反映出智者成熟的智慧。

---

remembrance *n.* 回忆；记忆

reverence *n.* 尊敬；敬意

envoy *n.* 使者；使节

extort *v.* 敲诈；强取；逼取

hour, as much as they had delighted the simplicity of his childhood.

When we speak of nature in this manner, we have a distinct but most poetical sense in the mind. We mean the *integrity* of impression made by *manifold* natural objects. It is this which distinguishes the stick of timber of the wood-cutter, from the tree of the poet. The charming landscape which I saw this morning, is *indubitably* made up of some twenty or thirty farms. Miller owns this field, Locke that, and Manning the *woodland* beyond. But none of them owns the landscape. There is a property in the horizon which no man has but he whose eye can integrate all the parts, that is, the poet. This is the best part of these men's farms, yet to this their warranty-deeds give no title.

若我们以这种方式论及自然，鲜明而诗意的感觉便会油然而生。我们所说的这种感觉指的是种种自然物体产生的整体感。因其如此才得以将伐木工人手下的木材和诗人笔下的树木区别开来。今晨迷天的景致无疑是二三十多个农场的结合。这片田地属于米勒，那片田地属于洛克，而远处那片林地则属于曼宁。然而风景却不属于其中任何一个。地平线处有种财富，只属于一种人，这种人能将视线所及之物融为一体，这便是诗人。这景致是其农场中最有价值之处，然而在地契中却无一席之地。

---

integrity *n.* 完整；完全　　　　　　manifold *adj.* 多样的；各种各样的
indubitably *adv.* 无疑地；确实地　　woodland *n.* 林地；林区

To speak truly, few adult persons can see nature. Most persons do not see the sun. At least they have a very *superficial* seeing. The sun *illuminates* only the eye of the man, but shines into the eye and the heart of the child. The lover of nature is he whose inward and outward senses are still truly adjusted to each other; who has retained the spirit of *infancy* even into the era of manhood. His intercourse with heaven and earth, becomes part of his daily food. In the presence of nature, a wild delight runs through the man, in spite of real sorrows. Nature says,—he is my creature, and maugre all his *impertinent* griefs, he shall be glad with me. Not the sun or the summer alone, but every hour and season yields its tribute of delight; for every hour and change corresponds to and authorizes a different

---

　　实话实说，成人中见过自然者寥寥无几。绝大多数并未见过太阳。至少其所见流于肤浅。太阳只能照亮成人的眼睛，却能照亮孩子的眼睛和心灵。热爱自然者可将内外感觉协调一致，步入成年时依然保持童真。他与天地的交流幻化成每日食粮的一部分。于自然面前，尽管也有悲苦，但仍有种狂喜贯彻身心。自然说，我是他的造物主，尽管他满怀忧伤，但和我在一起终将获得欢乐。令人愉悦者，不单是太阳和夏日，尚有每个时辰、每个季节。因为从令人窒息的正午到恐怖的午夜，每一时辰的嬗变都符合

---

superficial *adj.* 肤浅的；表面的　　　illuminate *v.* 照亮；照明
infancy *n.* 婴儿期；幼年　　　　　　　impertinent *adj.* 不礼貌的；莽撞的

state of the mind, from breathless noon to grimmest midnight. Nature is a setting that fits equally well a comic or a mourning piece. In good health, the air is a cordial of incredible virtue. Crossing a bare common, in snow puddles, at *twilight*, under a clouded sky, without having in my thoughts any occurrence of special good fortune, I have enjoyed a perfect *exhilaration*. I am glad to the brink of fear. In the woods too, a man casts off his years, as the snake his slough, and at what period soever of life, is always a child. In the woods, is perpetual youth. Within these plantations of God, a *decorum* and *sanctity* reign, a perennial festival is dressed, and the guest sees not how he should tire of them in a thousand years. In the woods, we return to reason and faith. There I feel that nothing can befall me in

---

或者赋予人不同的心境。自然是种环境，既适合上演喜剧，亦适合上演悲剧。身体健康之际，空气中也弥漫着难以置信的美德。黄昏时分，天空阴云密布，我穿过光秃秃的土地，立于雪洼中，心中无福祸降临之念，兴奋之情无以言表，即便此刻身处恐惧边缘，我亦欣然。驻足丛林亦是如此。人们如蛇之蜕皮，将年龄抛却，不论年纪几何，将永为孩童。人们将在林中青春永驻。在这上帝打造的林中，礼仪和圣洁统治一切，自然永着节日盛装，林中访客居千年而不觉厌倦。我们在林中回归理性和信仰。在那里，我终其一生都不会有不幸降临——没有耻辱、没有灾难（请这些远离

---

twilight *n.* 黄昏
decorum *n.* 得体；庄重；有礼

exhilaration *n.* 兴高采烈；兴奋
sanctity *n.* 神圣；圣洁

life, —no disgrace, no calamity, (leaving me my eyes,) which nature cannot repair. Standing on the bare ground, —my head bathed by the *blithe* air, and uplifted into infinite space, —all mean *egotism* vanishes. I become a transparent eye-ball; I am nothing; I see all; the currents of the Universal Being circulate through me; I am part or particle of God. The name of the nearest friend sounds then foreign and *accidental*: to be brothers, to be acquaintances, —master or servant, is then a trifle and a disturbance. I am the lover of uncontained and immortal beauty. In the wilderness, I find something more dear and connate than in streets or villages. In the *tranquil* landscape, and especially in the distant line of the horizon, man beholds somewhat as beautiful as his own nature.

The greatest delight which the fields and woods minister, is the suggestion of an occult relation between man and the vegetable. I

我的视线吧）。对于这种种不幸，大自然也束手无策。我站在空地上——思绪沐浴在欢乐的氛围中，飘飘然已至无极之境——卑鄙的一己之私销声匿迹。我幻化成透明的眼球、本身不复存在，却洞察一切。上帝的精气在我周身循环，我成为上帝的一部分，成为上帝的一颗微粒。于是挚友的名字听上去陌生而偶然：兄弟、熟人、主人、仆人霎时琐碎而烦恼起来。我爱这不羁之美，爱这不朽之美。我于旷野中觅得较之村落街道更珍贵、更密切之物。在这静谧的旷野中，尤其是在遥远的地平线上，人类看到如其天性般美丽之物。

　　田野和丛林馈赠的至上欢愉暗示着人类与植物之间有着某种神秘联系。我并不孤独、亦未被忽视。植物向我点头致意，我也向它们点头致

---

blithe *adj.* 快乐无忧的；欢乐的　　　　egotism *n.* 自我中心；自私自利
accidental *adj.* 偶然的；意外的　　　　tranquil *adj.* 平静的；宁静的

am not alone and unacknowledged. They nod to me, and I to them. The waving of the boughs in the storm, is new to me and old. It takes me by surprise, and yet is not unknown. Its effect is like that of a higher thought or a better emotion coming over me, when I deemed I was thinking justly or doing right.

Yet it is certain that the power to produce this delight, does not reside in nature, but in man, or in a *harmony* of both. It is necessary to use these pleasures with great temperance. For, nature is not always tricked in holiday *attire*, but the same scene which yesterday breathed perfume and glittered as for the *frolic* of the *nymphs*, is overspread with melancholy today. Nature always wears the colors of the spirit. To a man laboring under calamity, the heat of his own fire hath sadness in it. Then, there is a kind of contempt of the landscape felt by him who has just lost by death a dear friend. The sky is less grand as it shuts down over less worth in the population.

意。风暴中摇晃的树枝于我既陌生又熟悉。它让我惊讶却并不陌生。我自以为所思所做正确时，植物对我的影响好似更高尚的思想或更美好的情感将我征服。

　　诚然，产生这种欢愉的力量不在自然，而在人类，或者在两者的和谐统一。不过在享受欢愉之际仍需有所节制。因为自然并不总着节日盛装将自己装扮。昨日芳香四溢、熠熠生辉，恍如仙女嬉戏之境，今日却一片阴郁。自然总披着各色情绪的外衣。于苦难中劳作者而言，心中的熊熊怒火也饱含悲戚。刚刚痛失亲友者感觉周围景致也富含讥诮之味。为芸芸众生哀悼时，浩渺的苍穹也为之收敛起光彩。

---

harmony *n.* 和谐；和睦　　　　　　　　attire *n.* 服装；衣服
frolic *n.* 嬉戏；嬉闹　　　　　　　　　nymph *n.* 仙女

32

New Friend

— Jack London

Irresistible impulses seized him. He would be lying in camp, dozing lazily in the heat of the day, when suddenly his head would lift and his ears cock up, intent and listening, and he would spring, to his feet and *dash away*, and on and on, for hours, through the forest aisles and across the open spaces where the niggerheads bunched. He loved to run

新 朋 友
——杰克·伦敦

它有种无法抗拒的冲动。它会躺在营地上，在日头下懒懒地打着瞌睡，会突然抬起头、竖起耳朵，仔细聆听；会猛然跳起、疾奔而去，它跑呀，跑呀，穿过林中小径，越过一簇簇暗色植物丛覆盖的开阔地带，一连跑上几个小时。它喜欢跑到下面干涸的河道里，喜欢偷偷地爬进树丛去窥探小鸟的生活。它会在白天某个时候躺在灌木丛中看鹧

dash away 匆忙离开

down dry watercourses, and to creep and spy upon the bird life in the woods. For a day at a time he would lie in the *underbrush* where he could watch the *partridges* drumming and strutting up and down. But especially he loved to run in the dim twilight of the summer midnights, listening to the *subdued* and sleepy murmurs of the forest, reading signs and sounds as man may read a book, and seeking for the mysterious something that called—called, waking or sleeping, at all times, for him to come.

One night he sprang from sleep with a start, eager-eyed, nostrils quivering and scenting, his mane bristling in recurrent waves. From the forest came the call (or one note of it, for the call was many noted), distinct and definite as never before, —a long-drawn howl, like, yet unlike, any noise made by *husky* dog. And he knew it, in the old familiar way, as a sound heard before. He sprang through

---

鸪鸟拍打着翅膀、来来回回地昂首阔步。他尤其喜欢夏日的午夜在昏暗的蒙蒙夜色中奔跑，倾听大森林沉睡中温柔的呢喃，它像人们阅读书籍时一样，试图读懂那些符号、听懂那些声音、追寻那种神秘：那是一种呼唤，一种它或睡或醒时都在呼唤的声音。

　　一天晚上，它从睡梦中惊醒，双眼泛着热切的光泽。微颤的鼻孔仔细地嗅着，全身的毛发竖了起来，形成一层层波浪。森林深处又传来了那种呼唤（或是那种呼唤的一个音调，因为那种呼唤有多种音调），这次的呼唤：音色清晰，音调准确，以前从未听过——这是一种拖得很长的嗥叫，这嗥叫好像又不像爱斯基摩犬发出的声音。巴克知道这种嗥叫：这是一种古老的、熟悉的嗥叫，就像以前听过一样。巴克一跃而起，穿过沉睡的营

---

underbrush *n.* 灌木丛　　　　　　　　partridge *n.* 山鹑；鹧鸪
subdued *adj.* 柔和的；小声的　　　　　husky *n.* 爱斯基摩犬

the sleeping camp and in swift silence dashed through the woods. As he drew closer to the cry he went more slowly, with caution in every movement, till he came to an open place among the trees, and looking out saw, *erect* on *haunches*, with nose pointed to the sky, a long, lean, timber wolf.

He had made no noise, yet it ceased from its howling and tried to sense his presence. Buck stalked into the open, half crouching, body gathered compactly together, tail straight and stiff, feet falling with unwonted care. Every movement advertised commingled threatening and overture of friendliness. It was the *menacing truce* that marks the meeting of wild beasts that prey. But the wolf fled at sight of him. He followed, with wild leapings, in a frenzy to overtake. He ran him into a blind channel, in the bed of the creek where a timber jam barred

地，悄悄地快速冲过树林。它越是接近这声音，就走得越慢。它小心翼翼地迈着每一步，直到来到林中的一个开阔地带。它挺起腰来，抬头向前看去，原来是一只森林狼，正斜立着细长的身子，仰天长啸。

巴克没有弄出任何声音，可那只狼还是停止了嗥叫，感觉到了它的存在。巴克昂首阔步地走进了开阔地带，它半蹲着身子、身体收拢在一起、尾巴又直又硬、四肢异常小心地踏在地上。巴克的每一个动作都夹杂着恐吓和友好，这是一种捕食的野兽间濒于休战的表示。但是这只狼还是一看见它就逃跑了。巴克野性地跳跃着尾随着，狂暴地追赶着。巴克把那只狼赶进了一条黑黑的通道，在小河的河床上，一大堆木头拦住了去路。那只

erect *adj.* 直立的
menacing *adj.* 威胁的；威吓的

haunch *n.* 腰腿部
truce *n.* 休战

the way. The wolf whirled about, pivoting on his hind legs after the fashion of Joe and of all cornered husky dogs, *snarling* and bristling, clipping his teeth together in a continuous and rapid succession of snaps.

Buck did not attack, but Circled him about and *hedged* him in with friendly advances. The wolf was suspicious and afraid; for Buck made three of him in weight, while his head barely reached Buck's shoulder. Watching his chance, he darted away, and the chase was resumed. Time and again he was cornered, and the thing repeated, though he was in poor condition, or Buck could not so easily have overtaken him. He would run till Buck's head was even with his *flank*, when he would whirl around at bay, only to dash away again at the

---

狼旋转了起来，以两条后腿为轴心，用巴克以前队友乔的时髦动作，以及所有被逼到困镜中的爱斯基摩犬一样咆哮着，毛发高高竖起，龇着牙，不断快速地猛咬着。

巴克没有进攻，而是用一种友好的态度，围着它转圈。这只狼迟疑起来，害怕起来，因为巴克的身体足足是它的三倍，而它的脑袋只到巴克的肩膀。看见巴克过来了，它又猛地跑开了。追击又重新开始了。那狼三番两次被逼入困境，于是刚才发生的事情又重复起来。显然这狼状况不佳。否则，巴克也很难追上它。巴克的头一到它的侧面，它就跑开，逼入困境时就旋转起来，一有机会便迅速跑开。

---

snarl *v.* 咆哮　　　　　　　　　　hedge *v.* 用树篱围起

flank *n.* 侧面

first opportunity.

But in the end Buck's *pertinacity* was rewarded; for the wolf, finding that no harm was intended, finally sniffed noses with him. Then they became friendly, and played about in the nervous, half-coy way with which fierce beasts belie their fierceness. After some time of this the wolf started off at an easy *lope* in a manner that plainly showed he was going somewhere. He made it clear to Buck that he was to come, and they ran side by side through the sombre twilight, straight up the creek bed, into the gorge from which it issued, and across the bleak divide where it took its rise.

On the opposite slope of the *watershed* they came down into

但巴克的固执终于得到了回报。因为那狼用鼻子去闻，终于发现：巴克并不想伤害它。于是它们开始友好起来，它们收起野兽的凶猛劲儿，紧张地、半害羞地一起玩闹起来。这样过了一会儿，这只狼从容地大步慢跑起来，这显然是表示它要到什么地方去。它明白地向巴克表示它还要过来。于是它们肩并肩地穿过昏暗朦胧的夜色，径直跑上小河的河床，跑进小河流出的峡谷，跨过位于小河的发源地那荒凉的分水岭。

它们沿着小河的另一面斜坡跑下来，来到一个平坦的地方。这里有一

---

pertinacity *n.* 执拗；顽固
watershed *n.* 分水领；流域

lope *n.* 大步慢跑

a level country where were great stretches of forest and many streams, and through these great stretches they ran *steadily*, hour after hour, the sun rising higher and the day growing warmer. Buck was wildly glad. He knew he was at last answering the call, running by the side of his wood brother toward the place from where the call surely came. Old memories were coming upon him fast, and he was stirring to them as of old he stirred to the realities of which they were the shadows. He had done this thing before, somewhere in that other and *dimly* remembered world, and he was doing it again, now, running free in the open, the unpacked earth underfoot, the wide sky overhead.

片绵延不绝的森林，森林里有许多溪流。它们不慌不忙地跑过这片绵延的森林，跑了一小时又一小时。太阳越升越高，天气也越来越暖和。巴克欣喜若狂，它知道它终于在对那种"呼唤"做出回应了。它并肩和它森林中的兄弟朝着肯定发出呼唤声的地方跑去。旧时的记忆迅速向它袭来，它被惹起了兴致，渴望见一见这"呼唤"的影子，哪怕是鬼影也好。它以前做过这种事：是在一个什么地方，在一个隐约记得的世界里。现在它又在做这件事了。此刻，它脚下踏着未开垦的大地，头顶着辽阔的天空，自由自在地在野外奔跑着。

---

steadily *adv.* 稳步地；稳定地   dimly *adv.* 昏暗地；模糊地

They stopped by a running stream to drink, and, stopping, Buck remembered John Thornton. He sat down. The wolf started on toward the place from where the call surely came, then returned to him, *sniffing* noses and making actions as though to encourage him. But Buck turned about and started slowly on the back track. For the better part of an hour the wild brother ran by his side, whining softly. Then he sat down, pointed his nose upward, and *howled*. It was a *mournful* howl, and as Buck held steadily on his way he heard it grow faint and fainter until it was lost in the distance.

　　它们跑到一条潺潺的溪水边停下来，喝起了水。这时，巴克想起了约翰·桑顿，于是它便坐了下来。那狼朝着那个确实传来呼唤的地方跑去，然后又向巴克跑回来，用鼻子闻闻它，做出种种动作，仿佛是在鼓励它。但巴克却转过身来，开始慢慢往回走。它的野兄弟在它身旁跑着，陪着它走了一段美好的时光，这段时光里，对它反悔的举动轻轻地悲鸣着。接着它又坐了下来，仰天长嚎。这是悲伤的嗥叫……巴克坚定地走在了回家的路上。它听着那嚎叫声越来越模糊，直到消失在远方。

---

sniff *v.* 闻；嗅　　　　　　　　　　　　　　　howl *v.* 嗥叫；长嚎
mournful *adj.* 悲伤的；凄楚的

33

An Afternoon Walk in October

—— William Hale White

It was a day by itself, coming after a fortnight's storm and rain. The sun did not shine clearly, but it spread through the clouds a tender, *diffused* light, crossed by level cloud-bars, which stretched to a great length, quite *parallel*. The tints in the sky were wonderful, very *conceivable* shade of blue-grey, which contrived to *modulate* into the golden brilliance in which the sun

十月午后漫步
——威廉·黑尔·怀特

　　一连两周，狂风暴雨肆虐横行，这个晴天来得也就分外喜人。阳光并不十分明媚，穿过条条云彩变为柔和的光芒，四处抛洒，那云彩横跨长空，宛如一条条平行线向天际延伸。此时的天空精彩绝妙，青色灰色的云朵，浓淡不一，都在努力调整，试图变为遮于太阳脸庞的片片金光。午后，我信步出门。此时还不到一年中落叶纷飞的时节，花园却已是满地枯

diffuse *v.* 使（光线）漫射　　　　　　　　parallel *adj.* 平行的
conceivable *adj.* 可想到的；可想象的　　　　modulate *v.* 调整；调节

was veiled. I went out in the afternoon. It was too early in the year for a heavy fall of leaves, but nevertheless the garden was covered. They were washed to the sides of the roads, and lay heaped up over the road-gratings, masses of *gorgeous* harmonies in red, brown, and yellow. The *chestnuts* and *acorns* dropped in showers, and the patter on the gravel was a little weird. The chestnut husks split wide open when they came to the ground, revealing the polished brown of the shy fruit.

The lavish, drenching downpour in *extravagant* excess had been glorious. I went down to the bridge to look at the floods. The valley was a great lake, reaching to the big trees in the fields which had not yet lost the fire in their branches. The river-channel could be discerned only by the boiling of the current. It had risen above the

---

叶，它们被雨水冲到路边，堆叠于排水格栅之上，红色的、褐色的、黄色的，一团团、一簇簇，颜色如此绚烂，又如此协调。萧萧秋雨中被打落的栗子和橡果，噼噼啪啪打在砾石上，声音略带诡秘。栗子落地，外壳随即崩裂，露出油光光羞答答的褐色果肉。

　　连日来瓢泼如注的滂沱大雨留下了一幅壮观的景象。我走到桥头，观看雨后的洪流。此时的河谷俨然一片湖泽，水面漫及原野中高大的树木，枝头仍有天火的余烬。在奔流的洪水中，只能依稀辨出河道的轮廓。河水已经涨到石桥主拱洞的顶部，在那里回旋翻滚。被侧拱挡住去路的水流汹

---

gorgeous *adj.* 华丽的；绚丽的
acorn *n.* 橡子；橡（树果）实

chestnut *n.* 栗子
extravagant *adj.* 过度的；过分的

crown of the main stone arch, and swirled and plunged underneath it. A furious backwater, repulsed from the smaller arch, aided the tumult. The wind had gone and there was perfect silence, save for the *agitation* of the stream, but a few steps upwards the gentle tinkle of the little runnels could be heard in their deeply-cut, dark, and narrow channels. In a few minutes they were caught up, *rejoicing*, in the embrace of the deep river which would carry them with it to the sea. They were safe now from being lost in the earth.

I went a little further up the hill: a flock of about fifty sheep were crossing from a field on one side of the road to another directly opposite. They were packed close together, and then-backs were an undulating continuous surface. The *shepherd* was pursuing a stray sheep, and they stood still for a minute in the middle of the road.

涌倒流，让这幅画面更加惊心动魄。风已经停息，四周一片静寂，只剩河水的躁动之声。再上行几步，耳边便可响起小溪沿着幽深狭窄的河槽潺潺流动的声音。几分钟之后，它们就会欢快地投入那条河流的怀抱，随其流入大海，到时它们就安全了，不会再流失于土壤之中。

　　我继续朝山上走了一段，看见一群绵羊，五十只左右，正从路边一块田野穿过大路，走向正对面的另一块田野，它们紧紧簇拥在一起，绵软的后背连成一片，似波浪般高低起伏。牧羊人去追赶一只离群的羊，羊群一时停在了大路中央。此时一个农夫架着一辆双轮马车赶过来，被挡住了去

---

agitation　*n.* 煽动；鼓动　　　　　rejoice　*v.* 使欣喜；喜悦
shepherd　*n.* 牧羊人

A farmer came up in his gig and was held back. He used impatient language. Oh farmer! Which is of more importance to the heavenly power—that you should not be stopped, or that the sheep should *loiter* and go into that field at their own pace? All sheep, by the way, look sad. Perhaps they are dimly aware of their *destiny*.

It was about four o'clock. Two teams of plough-horses were coming out of a field on the way home. The owner takes great care of them. More *magnificent* horses never were seen; glossy coats, *tremendous* haunches, strong enough to shake a house if it came to an earnest pull, immense feet, show-stepping: very gentle the huge creatures seemed. The first team was led by a hale, ruddy-faced old man, between seventy and eighty, whom I have known for years.

路，他不耐烦地说了些粗暴的话。啊，农夫！对于万能的上帝来说，哪件事情会更重要呢——是你不该被拦下，还是羊群应该按照它们自己的节奏，慢慢悠悠地走向对面那块田野呢？顺便提一下，羊群里的每一只羊儿看起来都是愁容满面。或许，它们已经隐约知道自己将命归何处。

　　此时已是下午四点左右。两队耕完田的马儿正走出一块农田，踏上归家的路。马的主人对它们定是呵护备至，因为我从未见过如此俊美的马匹：毛皮油光闪亮；双胯肥硕健壮，情急之下狠命一拉，定能撼动一栋房子；四蹄巨大，却步履轻柔，看不出，这体型巨大的动物竟也十分温顺。第一队马儿由一个精神矍铄、满面红光的老汉牵引，老汉已经七八十岁了，与我相识多年，见面时总要乐呵呵地聊上几句。我说他应该为他的

---

loiter *v.* 闲逛；徘徊

magnificent *adj.* 宏伟的；壮丽的

destiny *n.* 命运

tremendous *adj.* 极大的

Always he has a cheery word for me. I told him he ought to be proud of such animals, and I am sure he is. He is happy on his eighteen shillings a week, looking neither before nor after, and knowing next to nothing of the world outside his village. Happy? Yes, and reasonably happy.

By the side of the second team marched a boy of about fifteen, with whip almost erect, over his shoulder. Put that boy back among his former *comrades*, the idlers in the village street, and he would be as unpleasant as any of them; but, entrusted with responsibility, he will pass through the middle of them, not knowing one.

I watched the procession through the *farmyard* gate, which slammed behind them, and, after leaning over it for a while, wandered homewards by the skirts of Hazel Wood just as the sun

---

马儿感到自豪，其实我也知道，他心中定有这感受。他虽每周只挣十八先令，既不回顾过去，也不展望未来，对村庄之外的世界一无所知，但却感到幸福。幸福吗？当然，而且是相当幸福。

走在第二队马儿旁边的是一个十五岁上下的少年，马鞭高高竖起，搭在肩头。如果让这少年重新回到他以前的同伴，那些在街头闲逛的小青年中去，他肯定一样招人讨厌，但现在却被委以重任，即便再次从他们中间走过，也会和他们形同陌路，不去理睬其中任何一个。

我看着马群走进了农场大院的大门，大门在他们身后随即砰然关上。我倚着门待了一会儿，然后在日落时分沿着赫兹尔树林外围漫步回家。林

---

comrade *n.* 朋友；忠实伙伴　　　　farmyard *n.* 农家庭院

was setting. The footpath goes along the edge of a field, two sides of which are bounded by trees, for the most part not very tall, but some of them are elms and rise to considerable height.

There is enough in a very common object to satisfy all our hunger—more than enough. I never leave the curve which limits the tops of the trees round that field without feeling that there is in it something which I cannot exhaust. The attraction is not the same as that of the "view" seen in passing. The "view" of a mountain peak or a waterfall is a surprise. I stay alone with my field for an hour or two and it *begets*, in addition to a growing sense of loveliness, a *religious* peace, victorious over trouble and doubts.

In 1814, before they were altered, the lines towards the end of the first book of the *Excursion* stood thus:

边那条小径紧挨一块农田，树木分列两侧，其中多数并不高大，但也有几棵榆树高高矗立。

每个平凡的景物都蕴涵着某种力量，能够满足我们的所有渴望——而且不止于此。每当我环顾田野四周，看到林木顶端绵延形成美丽的曲线，眼睛久久不能离开，总觉得其中有着某种魅力，是我所享用不尽的。这种魅力不同于旅途中看到的"风景"，山巅也好，飞瀑也好，是一种意外之喜，在这里，我却能独自一人，与我的田野厮守一两个小时，心中升腾起一种越来越强烈的美好感情，和内心虔诚的宁静之感，让我战胜一切烦恼和疑虑。

1814年，在《漫游》经修改之前，第一卷卷尾有这样几句：

---

beget *v.* 引起；导致　　　　　　　　　　religious *adj.* 虔诚的

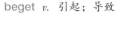

"those very plumes,

Those weeds, and the high spear-grass on that wall,

By mist and silent rain-drops silver'd o'er,

As once I passed, did to my heart convey

So still an image of *tranquility*,

So calm and still, and looked so beautiful

Amid the uneasy thoughts which filled my mind,

That what we feel of sorrow and despair

From ruin and from change, and all the grief

The passing shows of Being leave behind,

Appeared an *idle* dream, that could not live

Where *meditation* was."

"那些羽毛，那些野草，

还有墙头上那些高高的针茅，

裹着露水和无声的雨珠，银光闪耀，

每次经过，都在内心留下宁静祥和之兆，

这画面如此安详，如此美好；

愁绪充斥着我的大脑，

皆因毁灭与无常带来的悲伤和绝望，

和那让痛苦停留的飞逝过往，

此时却都幻化入一个无聊的梦乡，在冥想中变为空气般稀薄缥缈。"

---

tranquility *n.* 平静；安静　　　　　　　idle *adj.* 闲散的；琐碎无聊的

meditation *n.* 冥想；默想

34

To the Falls of Niagara

—— *Charles Dickens*

I had a desire to travel through the interior of the state of Ohio, and to "strike the lakes", as the phrase is, at a small town called Sandusky, to which that route would conduct us on our way to Niagara.

It was a *miserable* day; chilly and raw; a damp mist falling; and the trees in that northern region quite bare and *wintry*.

游尼亚加拉大瀑布

——查尔斯·狄更斯

我一直渴望能有机会到俄亥俄州境内去旅游，去一个名为桑达斯基的小镇感受一番"湖中戏水"之趣，同时，顺道也可去一趟尼亚加拉。

那日的天气简直糟透了，阴冷潮湿、迷雾浓重、几欲成滴；这季节北国的树木还是枝杈光秃，萧索一片。一路上，火车一停下来，我就会侧耳静听，希望能听到瀑布的吼声，同时我还不断地望向我所认定的瀑布所在

---

miserable *adj.* 苦恼的；令人难受的   wintry *adj.* 冬天的；寒冷的

Whenever the train halted, I listened for the roar; and was constantly straining my eyes in the direction where I knew the Falls must be, from seeing the river tolling on towards them; every moment expecting to behold the spray. Within a few minutes of our stopping, not before, I saw two great white clouds rising up slowly and *majestically* from the depths of the earth. That was all. At length we alighted: and then for the first time, I heard the mighty rush of water, and felt the ground tremble underneath my feet.

The bank is very steep, and was *slippery* with rain, and half-melted ice. I hardly know how I got down, but I was soon at the bottom, and climbing, with two English officers who were crossing and had joined me, over some broken rocks, deafened by the noise, half-blinded by the *spray*, and wet to the skin. We were at the foot of the American Fall. I could see an immense torrent of water tearing

---

的方向，我知道瀑布一定在那儿，因为滚滚河水正涌向那个方向；同时，我更是时刻期盼着飞溅的浪花出现。停车之前的几分钟内，我看到了两块云彩缓慢地从地心深处升腾起来，甚为壮观。这就是我车上所见。最后，我们下车了，终于，我第一次听到了激流迸射的声音，同时也感觉到脚下的大地都在震颤。

崖岸十分陡峭，因为刚刚下过雨，再加上化了一半的冰，地面上滑溜溜的。我都不知道我是怎么走下去的，但不一会儿，我就到了山脚下，同两个途中偶遇后又和我结伴而行的军官一起攀上了一片嶙峋的怪石堆，顷刻间，震耳欲聋之声扑来，激起水花四溅，几欲迷人眼，我们衣衫全湿。原来，是到了美国瀑布的脚下。只见，滔天巨浪，腾空而下，但这巨浪形

---

majestically *adv.* 宏伟地；壮丽地　　　　slippery *adj.* 滑溜溜的；滑的
spray *n.* 水花；飞沫

headlong down from some great height, but had no idea of shape, or situation, or anything but vague *immensity*.

When we were seated in the little ferry-boat, and were crossing the *swollen* river immediately before both cataracts, I began to feel what it was: but I was in a manner *stunned*, and unable to comprehend the vastness of the scene. It was not until I came on Table Rock, and looked—Great Heaven, on what a fall of bright-green water! —that it came upon me in its full might and majesty.

Then, when I felt how near to my Creator I was standing, the first effect, and the enduring one—instant and lasting—of the tremendous spectacle, was Peace. Peace of Mind, tranquillity,

---

状如何，从何而来，我全无概念，只觉出渺茫一片。

随后，我们乘上了小渡船，在经过紧贴两个大瀑布前的汹涌的河流时，我才开始明白是怎么回事：但我却有些目眩，无法领会到面前的场景有多么壮观。直到我到达了平顶岩上，远眺时——天哪，那是怎样的一片飞流直下的碧波呀！——此时，它的宏伟与浩瀚之美方才完全呈现在了我面前。

于是，我感觉到我与造物者之间的距离是如此之近，那恢宏的景观，带给我的一瞬间的印象，也是永恒的印象——瞬间却持久——是平静：内

---

immensity *n.* 无限；广大　　　　　swollen *adj.* （河水）上涨的；湍流的
stun *v.* 使眩晕；使目瞪口呆

calm recollections of the Dead, great thoughts of Eternal Rest and Happiness: nothing of gloom or terror. Niagara was at once stamped upon my heart, an Image of Beauty; to remain there, changeless and *indelible*, until its pulses cease to beat, for ever.

Oh, how the strife and trouble of daily life receded from my view, and *lessened* in the distance, during the ten memorable days we passed on that Enchanted Ground! What voices spoke from out the thundering water; what faces, faded from the earth, looked out upon me from its gleaming depths; what Heavenly promise *glistened* in those angels' tears, the drops of many hues, that showered around, and twined themselves about the gorgeous arches which the

---

心的平静，对逝者淡淡的安详的回忆，对永久的安宁和幸福的无限展望，没有丝毫阴郁或惶恐之意。只一瞬间，尼亚加拉已深深地刻在了我的心里——那么美好的形象，它会永远留在我的心中，不会改变亦不会消失，直到我心跳停止。

在那梦幻般的国度里，我们度过了毕生难忘的十天，那段日子里，日常生活中的纷争与烦恼逐渐离我远去，消失在远方！震耳欲聋的巨浪声是那么的动人心魄；退隐于尘世却又从碧波闪耀中望向我的，是哪般的面目啊；在变幻莫测、横亘半空的绚烂彩虹周围，天使的泪滴闪现着怎样的神殿旨意，又是怎样的五彩纷呈、珠圆玉润啊！

---

indelible *adj.* 难以去除的；难忘的

glisten *v.* 闪光；闪耀

lessen *v.* 使减少；使缩小

changing rainbows made!

I never *stirred* in all that time from the Canadian side, whither I had gone at first. I never crossed the river again; for I knew there were people on the other shore, and in such a place it is natural to shim strange company. To wander to and fro all day, and see the *cataracts* from all points of view; to stand upon the edge of the great Horse-Shoe Fall, marking the hurried water gathering strength as it approached the *verge*, yet seeming, too, to pause before it shot into the gulf below; to gaze from the river's level up at the torrent as it came streaming down; to climb the neighbouring heights and watch it through the trees, and see the wreathing water in the rapids hurrying on to take its fearful plunge; to linger in the shadow of the

---

从我一到那儿开始，我就待在加拿大瀑布那边，十天以来一直如此。我再没有乘船过河；因为我知道，河的那边也有人，而且，在这种地方，最好还是避免和陌生人等纠缠在一起。整日都徘徊在瀑布四周，从各个角度来欣赏尼亚加拉大瀑布；站在马蹄铁大瀑布边上，注视着湍急的洪流，铆足了劲儿一般，直冲岸边，却又好像在投入湾底之前，稍稍停顿了一下似的；沿河面往上看去，巨浪奔涌，一泻千里；登上瀑布的邻岭，从树梢树丛的间隙中望过去，激流盘旋而前，旋转而下，猛然跃入深渊；藏身于下游三英里处的巨石旁，看向河水，漩涡起伏似有应答，表面上看不出

---

stir *v.* 移动；离开
verge *n.* 边缘；界限

cataract *n.* 大瀑布

solemn rocks three miles below; watching the river as, stirred by no visible cause, it heaved and eddied and awoke the *echoes*, being troubled yet, far down beneath the surface, by its giant leap; to have Niagara before me, lighted by the sun and by the moon, red in the day's decline, and grey as evening slowly fell upon it; to look upon it everyday, and wake up in the night and hear its ceaseless voice: this was enough.

I think in every quiet season now, still do those waters roll and leap, and roar and *tumble*, all daylong; still are the rainbows spanning them, a hundred feet below. Still, when the sun is on them, do they shine and glow like molten gold. Still, when the day is *gloomy*, do they fall like snow, or seem to crumble away like the front of a great

---

来它涌动的原因，实则是因为水底深处有巨浪在翻滚；我的目光终日不离尼亚加拉，看着它在日光下涌动华彩，看着她在月光中微波闪亮，夕阳西下一片红，暮色苍茫灰蒙蒙；白天，满眼里看到的都是它，晚上，辗转时耳中听到的也是它：对我来讲，这已足够。

　　现如今，平静下来的时刻，我总忍不住回想：那片浩瀚的洪流是否依旧奔腾怒吼；虹霓是否依旧横跨于其下一百英尺的空中。阳光闪耀时，它是否依旧如金波玉液般晶莹明澈。天气阴沉时，它是否依旧像纯洁的飞雪般纷纷而下；或者如细末般从岩壁上簌簌剥落；抑或如棉絮状的浓烟，从山腹里喷涌而出。但这浩瀚的洪流啊，从天而降之时，总好似要奔赴死

---

echo n. 回声；回响　　　　　　　　　tumble v. （水）冲刷；滚滚流过
gloomy adj. 昏暗的

chalk cliff; or roll down the rock like dense white smoke. But always does the mighty stream appear to die as it comes down, and always from its *unfathomable* grave arises that tremendous ghost of spray and mist which is never laid: which has haunted this place with the same dread solemnity since Darkness brooded on the deep, and that first flood before the Deluge—Light—came rushing on Creation at the word of God.

亡一般，从它那深不可测的水墓中升腾出了浪花和迷雾的巨大幽魂，永不可降服：在黑暗还统治深渊之时，在第一次洪流到来之前，在光芒还未接受上帝命令弥漫宇宙之前，它就已经统治了这整片领地，如神灵般庄严圣洁。

---

unfathomable *adj.* 高深莫测的；深奥的

35

A Night Among the Pines

— Robert Louis Stevenson

A faint wind, more like a moving coolness than a stream of air, passed down the glade from time to time; so that even in my great *chamber* the air was being renewed all night long. I thought with horror of the inn at Chasserades and the congregated *nightcaps*, with horror of the *nocturnal* prowesses of clerks and students, of hot theatres and pass-keys

夜宿松林
——罗伯特·路易斯·史蒂文森

阵阵柔风不时拂过林间空地，与其用气流来形容它，倒不如用"流动的凉意"来得更贴切些；即使裹在我的睡袋里，整晚也都能享受到流动的清新的空气。每当回忆起切斯雷德的小旅馆和那攒到一处的许多睡帽们，回忆起那些伙计们和学生们整夜的喧闹，还有闷热的剧院，万能钥匙和紧挨在一起的房间，我都感到非常恐怖。难得现在能享受这般宁静的独处时光，这般超然物外。虽说，我们常常从户外的世界蜷

chamber *n.* 大房间
nocturnal *adj.* 夜间的

nightcap *n.* 睡帽

and close rooms. I have not often enjoyed a more serene possession of myself, nor felt more independent of material aids. The outer world, from which we cower into our houses, seemed after all a gentle habitable place; and night after night a man's bed, it seemed, was laid and waiting for him in the fields, where God keeps an open house. I thought I had rediscovered one of those truths which are revealed to *savages* and hid from political economists: at the least, I had discovered a new pleasure for myself. And yet even while I was *exulting* in my solitude I became aware of a strange lack. I wished a companion to be near me in the starlight, silent and not moving, but ever within touch. For there is a *fellowship* more quiet even than

縮回自己的屋中去，但户外世界似乎始终是个宜居之地；夜复一夜，在野外，在上帝开阔的房屋中，似乎已安放好了一张大床，等待着人类的到来。我自觉自己重新发现了大自然无数真理中的一条——对此，村夫莽汉早已知晓，但政治经济学家们却尚未悟出：最起码，我为自己发掘出了一种新的乐趣。然而，我在享受独处的乐趣时，却也奇怪地感觉到心中还有缺憾在。多么希望，在这样的星光璀璨下，能有个伴儿躺在我近旁，不说，不动，却永远触手可及。因为，有种情谊，比独处更能给人带来内心的恬静，确切地说，这才是独处的完美境界。能与自己心爱的女子同在户外生活，在各种生活方式中，是最完美、最自由的那种了。

savage *n.* 野蛮人；残暴的人　　　　　　exult *v.* 狂喜；欢欣鼓舞
fellowship *n.* 友谊；交情

solitude, and which, rightly understood, is solitude made perfect. And to live out of doors with the woman a man loves is of all lives the most complete and free.

As I thus lay, between *content* and *longing*, a faint noise stole towards me through the pines. I thought, at first, it was the crowing of cocks or the barking of dogs at some very distant farm; but steadily and gradually it took articulate shape in my ears, until I became aware that a passenger was going by upon the high-road in the *valley*, and singing loudly as he went. There was more of good-will than grace in his performance; but he trolled with ample lungs; and the sound of his voice took hold upon the hillside and set the

---

我就这样躺着，心中有满足也有期许。这时，一丝缥缈的声音透过松林隐隐传至耳畔，刚开始，我还以为是远处农庄中的鸡鸣狗吠之声，但慢慢地，它变得愈加清晰起来，我才意识到原来是在谷中的大路上，有个赶路人在边走边高声歌唱。歌声虽不是很动听，但听来却十分亲切。他中气十足，歌声荡漾在山坡上，连这青葱幽谷间的空气都被激荡起来了。我曾听到夜晚沉睡的城市中，行人匆匆赶路的声音；有些人也会唱歌；记得还有个人曾响亮地吹着风笛。我还听到，在数小时的静谧后，霍然响起的马

---

content　*n.*　满足

longing　*n.*　渴望；热望

valley　*n.*　山谷；溪谷

air shaking in the leafy *glens*. I have heard people passing by night in sleeping cities; some of them sang; one, I remember, played loudly on the bagpipes. I have heard the rattle of a cart or carriage spring up suddenly after hours of stillness, and pass, for some minutes, within the range of my hearing as I lay abed. There is a romance about all who are abroad in the black hours, and with something of a thrill we try to guess their business. But here the romance was double: first, this glad passenger, lit internally with wine, who sent up his voice in music through the night; and then I, on the other hand, buckled into my *sack*, and smoking alone in the pine-woods between four and five thousand feet towards the stars.

车的吱嘎声，当时我醒着躺在床上，感觉数分钟过后，远去的马车声还隐约回响在耳边。夜晚时，所有还在外活动的人都会给人神秘莫测的感觉，人们会激动地猜测他们到底在干什么。现在，这儿便有着双重的神秘感：一重是这位快乐的赶路人，酒意陶然，放声歌唱；另一重，则是躺在睡袋里的我，独自抽着烟，仰望着上方四五千英尺之遥的繁星满天。

---

glen *n.* 峡谷　　　　　　　　　　　　　　　　sack *n.* 大口袋

36

The Assabeth

— *Nathaniel Hawthorne*

Blessed was the sunshine when it came again at the close of another stormy day, beaming from the edge of the western horizon; while the massive *firmament* of clouds threw down all the gloom it could, but served only to kindle the golden light into a more brilliant glow by the strongly contrasted shadows. Heaven smiled at the earth, so long

亚沙白溪

——纳撒尼尔·霍桑

感谢上天，在又一天的风雨阴霾后，阳光终于到来，再次闪耀在西方地平线上。天空中依旧密布着层层阴云，但它散发出的重重阴霾，在清晰地明暗对比中，却使得这缕金光更显夺目亮丽。虽然天空的眼睛依旧微闭着，但它已向大地露出了笑脸，那真是久违的笑容啊！明天，又可以踏足高山丛林间了。

---

firmament *n.* 天空；苍穹

unseen, from beneath its heavy *eyelid*. Tomorrow for the hill-tops and the wood-paths.

Or it might be that Ellery Channing came up the avenue to join me in a fishing excursion on the river. Strange and happy times were those when we cast aside all *irksome* forms and strait-laced habitudes, and delivered ourselves up to the free air, to live like the Indians or any less conventional race during one bright *semicircle* of the sun. Rowing our boat against the current, between wide *meadows*, we tinned aside into the Assabeth. A more lovely stream than this, for a mile above its unction with Concord, has never flowed on earth, —nowhere, indeed, except to lave the interior regions of a poet's

---

　　也有可能艾勒立·钱宁会出现在大街上与我一同去河边钓鱼。回想过去，真是奇妙快活的日子啊！那时，我们会抛却一切令人憋闷窒息的客套礼俗，去野外尽情游玩，日出日落，我们就像个印第安人或不受传统习俗约束的人那般过着日子。小舟逆流而上，穿行过两岸宽阔的草原，我们便折入了亚沙白溪。在这河水与康谷河汇合点上游一英里处，景色如此秀丽，除却涤荡着诗人心灵的神溪之外，这般迷人的溪流这世上怕再也找不到第二条了。周边的丛林山峰是天然的避风屏障，外边即便是狂风扫过，这里幽暗的水面也少见一丝波纹。溪流迂回荡漾，轻轻巧巧，好似舟人心中念想，便可使小舟溯洄直上。小舟轻巧前行，穿过密林深处，林叶籁籁

---

eyelid *n.* 眼睑；眼皮　　　　　　　irksome *adj.* 令人厌烦的；令人烦恼的
semicircle *n.* 半圆；半圆弧　　　　meadow *n.* 草地；牧场

imagination. It is sheltered from the breeze by woods and hillside; so that elsewhere there might be a hurricane, and here scarcely a ripple across the shaded water. The current lingers along so gently that the mere force of the boatman's will seems sufficient to *propel* his craft against it. It comes flowing softly through the midmost privacy and deepest heart of a wood which whispers it to be quiet; while the stream whispers back again from its *sedgy* borders, as if river and wood were hushing one another to sleep. Yes; the river sleeps along its course and dreams of the sky and of the clustering *foliage*, amid which fall showers of broken sunlight, imparting specks of vivid cheerfulness, in contrast with the quiet depth of the prevailing tint. Of all this scene, the slumbering river has a dream picture in its bosom.

作响，叮咛溪流切勿高声；而溪流，从莎草茂密的两岸上又做出了轻声应答，仿佛林木与溪流彼此安抚，嘘之入梦。是啊，溪流静静悄悄，安然前行，似在梦中，拥有着那片碧蓝晴空，拥有着那片枝繁叶茂，束束阳光从密叶缝隙中透出，点点晶莹，洒落满地；其旁便是碧波，宁静深邃，碧色一片，如此鲜明的对比，使林间的一切都变得生动欢快起来。所有的这些如画般的风景，都在安睡的溪流的心中，都在它的梦中。但是，梦中的和现实的风景——到底哪个才是更加真实的？——是我们那颗世俗的心清晰感觉到的？还是深邃的溪流中那神秘的幻象？当然，那种不受实体束缚的

---

propel *v.* 推进；推动　　　　　　　　sedgy *adj.* 莎草茂密的；莎草的
foliage *n.* （植物的）叶；枝叶

Which, after all, was the most real—the picture, or the original? —the objects palpable to our grosser senses, or their apotheosis in the stream beneath? Surely the disembodied images stand in closer relation to the soul. But both the original and the reflection had here an ideal charm; and had it been a thought more wild, I could have fancied that this river had strayed forth out of the rich scenery of my companion's inner world; only the vegetation along its banks should then have had an Oriental character.

Gentle and *unobtrusive* as the river is, yet the *tranquil* woods seem hardly satisfied to allow it passage. The trees are rooted on the very verge of the water, and dip their *pendent* branches into it. At one spot there is a lofty bank, on the slope of which grow some *hemlocks* declining across the stream and outstretched arm, as if resolute to

---

意象该是更加贴近我们灵魂的吧。但是，真实也好，幻象也罢，都有它们的极致之美；知此念想，或许有些离奇，我不禁幻想，这溪流也许是从我身旁那位胸怀宽广的友人心中生出的吧，蜿蜒曲折，流淌至此。若真是如此，那两岸的景致该再添上一些东方魅力才好。

溪流虽是可亲且无碍，但寂静的林木却似乎并不太乐意它从此穿行经过。林间树木大多扎根水畔，枝条下垂，浸入水中。那一处，是高高的岸崖，斜坡上生长着凡株铁杉，它们伸长着枝杈，斜倚在水面上，做出跳水之状。在他处，岸面和水面几近一体，连成片的树木，根部都已浸入水中，树冠树叶都几欲临近水面。山梗菜燃起它螺旋状的火焰，照亮着灌木

---

unobtrusive *adj.* 不引人注目的；不容易被注意到的

pendent *adj.* 吊着的；下垂的

tranquil *adj.* 宁静的

hemlock *n.* 铁杉木

take the plunge. In other places the banks are almost on a level with the water; so that the quiet congregation of trees set their feet in the flood, and are fringed with foliage down to the surface. Cardinal flowers kindle their spiral flames and illuminate the dark nook among the *shrubbery*. The pond-lily grows abundantly along the margin—that delicious flower, which, as Thoreau tells me, opens its virgin bosom to the first sunlight and perfects its being through the magic of that *genial* kiss. He has beheld beds of them unfolding in due succession as the sunrise stole gradually from flower to flower—a sight not to be hoped for unless when a poet adjust his inward eye to a proper focus with the outward organ. Grape-vines here and there *twine* themselves around shrub and tree and hang their clusters over the water within reach of the boatman's hand. Oftentimes they unite

丛里的幽暗角落。紧邻溪边，荷花大片地盛开着——这娇艳欲滴的花朵啊，正如梭罗告诉我的，在阳光初照后才会展开她的处女般的胸怀，又会在阳光亲抚的神奇力量下，如少女般长大成熟起来。这风景，他曾多次见到过，阳光依次所到之处，荷花就会一一绽放——可这般美景，若不是诗人能灵敏地感知并向我们描述出来，我们还真不可能会见到。葡萄更是随处可见，藤条爬满了包括灌木丛在内的各种树木，有的上面还悬着长串颗粒，舟人经过，伸手便可摘了去。时常地，这些藤条也会将本不属于同一种类的两株树木，如铁杉与枫树，硬是缠绕在一起，逃都逃不开，且为了一切美满，还会把自己紫色的后代送去给它们做儿女。其间有一株藤条，

shrubbery *n.* 灌木丛   genial *adj.* 亲切的；友善的
twine *n.* 盘绕；缠绕在一起的东西

two trees of alien race in an *inextricable* twine, marrying the hemlock and the maple against their will, and enriching them with a purple offspring of which neither is the parent. One of these ambitious parasites has climbed into the upper branches of a tall, white pine, and is still ascending from bough to bough, unsatisfied till it shall crown tree's airy summit with a wreath of its broad foliage and a cluster of its grapes.

The winding course of the stream continually shut out the scene behind us, and revealed as calm and lovely a one before. We glided from depth to depth, and breathed new *seclusion* at every turn. The shy king-fisher flew from the withered branch close at hand to another at a distance, uttering a *shrill* cry of anger or alarm. Ducks that had been floating there since the preceding eve were startled at our approach, and skimmed along the glassy river, breaking its dark

---

虽已依附于树木上，却有着更远大的志向，它已攀到了一棵高耸入云的白皮松的顶端枝杈上，而且还一枝一枝地缠绕上去，直到它能把自己的簇簇叶片和串串果实高挂到树冠为止。

溪流蜿蜒前行，面前的景色便一一向后退去，但迎面而来的景致也一样宁静可爱。我们继续向溪流深处划过去，每次转弯后，都感觉到愈加幽僻。一只羞涩的翠鸟突然在我们近旁的一枯枝上扑腾着飞起，落到了远一些的枝上，还伴着一声尖细的鸣叫，不知是受惊了还是有些怒意。已在这儿留宿一夜的野鸭也被我们的到来吓到了，快速划过了明镜般的水面，深邃的水面霎时泛起了明亮的波纹。成片的睡莲中不时有小梭鱼跃起。在岩石或树根处悠闲地沐浴阳光的乌龟也突然跳起，跃入水中。岸边波心的景

---

inextricable *adj.* 分不开的；解不开的　　　seclusion *n.* 隔绝；隐居
shrill *adj.* （声音）刺耳的；尖厉的

surface with a bright streak. The pickerel leaped from among the lilypads. The turtle, sunning itself upon a rock or at the root of a tree, slid suddenly into the water with a plunge. The painted Indian who paddled his *canoe* along the Assabeth three hundred years ago could hardly have seen a wilder gentleness displayed upon its banks and reflected in its bosom than we did. Nor could the same Indian have prepared his noontide meal with more simplicity. We drew up our *skiff* at some point where the over-arching shade formed a natural bower, and there kindled a fire with the pine cones and decayed branches that lay *strewn* plentifully around. Soon the smoke ascended among the trees, impregnated with a savory incense, not heavy, dull, and surfeiting, like the stream of cookery within doors, but sprightly and *piquant*. The smell of our feast was akin to the woodland odors with which it mingled: there was no sacrilege committed by our intrusion

色粗犷中也不乏妩媚。如果一个文身画面的印第安人三百年前乘小舟从此处经过的话，他见到的景色应该也不会比我们如今见到的更惊艳。此外，他烧的午饭也不会比我们的更简单了。后来，我们到了一处枝丫交错，树荫浓密的地方，便停舟上岸了。捡拾了些周围随处可见的松果败枝，生起火来。霎时，烟柱升腾起来，直冲树梢，但烟火环绕中却充满了一股香气，让人神清气爽，并不同于我们平日室内厨房中所充斥的那种浓重、浑浊、让人憋闷的气息。午餐的香味与林地间的气息融合在一起：我们擅入此地倒也不算是对幽静景致的亵渎，这儿虽然神圣静寂，但却也热情洋溢，并非拒人于千里之外，所以我们可以自如地在此点火烧饭，尽情享

canoe *n.* 独木舟；小划子
strewn *adj.* 布满的；撒满的

skiff *n.* 小艇；小船
piquant *adj.* 刺激的；令人兴奋的

there: the sacred solitude was hospitable, and granted us free leave to cook and eat in the recess that was at once our kitchen and banqueting hall. It is strange what humble offices may be performed in a beautiful scene without destroying its poetry. Our fire, red gleaming among the trees, and we beside it, busied with culinary rites and spreading out our meal on a moss-grown log, all seemed in unison with river gliding by and foliage rustling over us. And, what was strangest, neither did our *mirth* seem to disturb the propriety of the *solemn* woods; although the *hobgoblins* of the old wilderness and the will-of-the-wisps that glimmered in the marshy places might have come trooping to share our table-talk, and have added their shrill laughter to our table-talk, and have added their shrill laughter to our *merriment*. It was the very spot in which to utter the extremest

---

用，把这整片的浓荫绿树视作我们的厨房餐厅。稀奇的是，在如此美好的景色中，大吃特吃，谈笑风生，看起来也并没有大煞风景。林中热烈燃烧的火苗，近旁忙碌烹调忙碌上菜的我们，甚至是作为我们餐桌的那根满是苔藓的伐木，所有的一切似乎都已与身边汩汩流过的溪水和上空簌簌而动的林叶深深地融为了一体。尤为稀奇的是，我们的欢乐嬉闹好像也没有影响到林间庄严肃穆的气氛；尽管这片古老粗犷的土地上的精灵和沼泽湿地里的磷火都可能成群到来，加入我们的热情讨论，尽管它们会使这里更加笑声不断，更加欢乐无比。在这里，你所倾诉的可以是最无厘头的，也可以是最深奥难懂的，或者是二者兼而有之的，或者是亦此亦彼的，全都在于聆听人的思想与感悟罢了。

---

mirth *n.* 欢笑；欢乐
hobgoblin *n.* （民间传说中的）淘气的小妖精

solemn *adj.* 严肃的；庄严的
merriment *n.* 欢笑；欢乐

nonsense or the profoundest wisdom, or that ethereal product of the mind which partakes of both, and may become one or the other, in correspondence with the faith and insight of the auditor.

So amid sunshine and shadow, rustling leaves and sighing waters, up gushed our talk like the *babble* of a *fountain*. The *evanescent* spray was Ellrery's; and his, too, the lumps of golden thought that lay glimmering in the fountain's bed and brightened both our faces by the reflection. Could he have drawn out that virgin gold and stamped it with the mint mark that alone gives currency, the world might have had the profit, and he the fame. My mind was the richer merely by the knowledge that it was there. But the chief profit of those wild days to him and me lay, not in any definite idea, not in any angular or rounded truth, which we dug out of the shapeless mass of problematical stuff, but in the freedom which we thereby

---

在灿烂阳光，摇曳树荫，沙沙林叶和汩汩流水中，我们的话题和思绪不禁变得如涌泉般，绵延而来。艾勒立的思绪虽会瞬间转变或消失，但却也好似璀璨的泉眼中那灿灿的金底，将我们的脸映照得满是明亮光辉。如果他能把里面的真金提炼出来，盖上造币厂的官方印章，像货币般发行开来，整个世界都会因其而获利，他也必将因此而声名鹊起。知道我的好友如此有天分，仅此一点，已让我的内心颇感充实了。在那些放浪形骸的日子里，我们最大的收获并不在于提出了什么具体的见解，也不在于从很多模棱两可难以琢磨的问题中找出了或是生硬或是丰满的所谓道理。而主要在于我们因此获得了自由，挣脱了一切习俗与传统，挣脱了人带给人的那种禁锢之感。今天既已如此自由，明日就不可能再重新做回"奴隶"了。

---

babble *n.* 含混不清的话；胡言乱语

evanescent *adj.* 逐渐消失的

fountain *n.* 喷泉

won from all custom and conventionalism and fettering influences of man on man. We were so free today that it was impossible to be slaves again tomorrow. When we crossed the threshold of the house or trod the thronged pavements of a city, still the leaves of the trees that *overhang* the Assabeth were whispering to us, "Be free! Be free!" therefore along that shady riverbank there are spots, marked with a heap of ashes and half-consumed brands, only less sacred in my remembrance than the hearth of a household fire.

And yet how sweet, as we floated homeward adown the golden river at sunset, —how sweet was it to return within the system of human society, not as to a *dungeon* and a chain, but as to a stately edifice, whence we could go forth at will into statelier simplicity!

当我们跨进家宅门槛或行走于城市间熙熙攘攘的人行道上时，亚沙白溪那沙沙的林叶也会在我们的耳畔响起，悄声说着"要自由！要自由！"。正因如此，林荫溪畔我们踏足的那些地方，那些餐后的堆堆灰烬，那些未吃完的食物，在我心中都变得愈加神圣，不亚于我们对家庭炉火所持有的那种神圣之感。

夕阳西下，溪面泛起了金光，景色异常迷人，我们将小舟掉转后，顺流而下，去往家的方向——回到那也算迷人的人类社会的规章制度中去，不过那里将不再有令人不快的束缚感，那里将是一座庄严的宅邸，在其间，我们能够随性而行，能够过上一种更加庄严却又简单的日子！此外，从河面上望向这座古宅，真是倍感亲切，绿柳覆荫，一切都淹没在果园与

---

overhang *v.* 悬于……之上   dungeon *n.* 地牢；土牢

How gently, too, did the sight of the Old Manse best seen from the river, over-shadowed with its willow and all environed about with the foliage of its orchard and avenue, —how gently did its gray, homely aspect *rebuke* the *speculative extravagances* of the day! It had grown sacred in connection with the artificial life against which we *inveighed*, it had been a home too; and, with these thoughts, it seemed to me that all the artifice and conventionalism of life was but an impalpable thinness upon its surface, and that the depth below was none the worse for it. Once, as we turned our boat to the bank, there was a cloud, in the shape of an immensely gigantic figure of a hound, couched above the house, as if keeping guard over it. Gazing at this symbol, I prayed that the upper influences might long protect the institutions that had grown out of the heart of mankind.

便道的枝繁叶茂苍翠欲滴之中——它那色调沉稳，平凡普通的外表，对于当下的投机取巧，奢靡浮华又何尝不是一种温和的斥责呢？在与我们所抨击的虚饰生活的息息相关中，这座宅邸便愈发显得神圣了！但它同时也是我们的家啊！想到这些，我恍然大悟，人生的所有诡计狡诈与墨守成规只不过是附着在其表面上的一层薄薄的无形的外壳罢了，底层深刻的东西并不一定会受到它多大的影响。曾有一次，我们将小舟靠向岸边时，发现天空中有一团乌云，形似巨型猎狗，蹲伏在宅邸上空，好似在守护着它。眼见此景，我便虔诚祈祷，祷告上苍能多加护佑那些顺应民意且深得民心的国家。

---

rebuke *v.* 指责
extravagance *n.* 奢侈；铺张

speculative *adj.* 投机的
inveigh *v.* 猛烈抨击；激烈反对

37

Flowery Tuscany

— David Herbert Lawrence

North of the Alps, the everlasting winter is interrupted by summers that struggle and soon yield; south of the Alps, the everlasting summer is interrupted by *spasmodic* and *spiteful* winters that never get a real hold, but that are mean and dogged. The in-between, in either case, is just as it may be. But the lands of the sun are south of the Alps, forever.

花季托斯卡纳
——戴维·赫伯特·劳伦斯

阿尔卑斯山以北，长时间的冬季迎来了夏季的挑战，但终因不敌，夏季很快便退去了。以南，长时间的夏季被间歇性的、满怀敌意的冬季所扰，但冬季永远也不可能成为主旋律，虽然它很恶毒也很顽抗。在两者的抗衡过程中，任何一种情形的出现，都只是种可能。但可以说，阿尔卑斯山以南，永远都是阳光明媚。

spasmodic *adj.* 间歇的；间断的   spiteful *adj.* 恶意的；怀恨的

In the morning, the sun shines strong on the horizontal green cloud-puffs of the pines, the sky is clear and full of life, the water runs *hastily*, still browned by the last juice of crushed olives. And there the earth's bowl of *crocuses* is amazing. You cannot believe that the flowers are really still. They are open with such delight, and their *pistil* thrust is so red-orange, and they are so many, all reaching out wide and *marvelous*, that it suggests a perfect ecstasy of radiant, thronging movement, lit-up violet and orange, and surging in some invisible rhythm of concerted, delightful movement. You cannot believe they do not move, and make some sort of crystalline sound of delight. If you sit still and watch, you begin to move with them, like moving with the stars, and you feel the sound of their radiance. All the little cells of the flowers must be leaping with flowery life and

---

　　清晨，强烈的阳光照射在远方松林的绿色云团上，天空澄明，生机无限。水流湍急，落入水中的碎橄榄将水涂抹成了棕褐色。铺满地面的番红花更是迷人一景。你不会相信那些花朵是真正静止不动的，它们那么欢欣地绽放开来，从花心中探出头来的雌蕊又透出那么让人倍感温暖的橘色。花朵不计其数，竞相开放，争奇斗艳，让人目眩神迷。成片的花朵摇曳起舞，紫色和橘色交织其间，像伴着一首首无声的动感乐曲似的。你不得不相信这些花朵是在舞动着的，不得不相信它们发出了水晶般透明的欢快的声音。如果你安静地坐下来，仔细观赏的话，你就会随着它们一起摆动起来，就像星星走你也走一样；你也会听到花朵们的灿烂光辉所带来的无限欢乐的声响，它们身上的每一个小小细胞上都洋溢着如花般的生命，都跳动着美丽的音符。

---

hastily *adv.* 急速地；仓促地　　　　　crocus *n.* 〈植〉番红花
pistil *n.* 〈植〉雌蕊　　　　　　　　　marvelous *adj.* 引起惊异的；非凡的

utterance.

And now that it is March, there is a rush of flowers. Down by the other stream, which turns sideways to the sun, and tangles the *brier* and *bramble*, down where the *hellebore* has stood so wan and dignified all winter, there are now white tufts of primroses, suddenly come. Among the tangle and near the water-lip, tufts and bunches of primroses, in abundance. Yet they look more wan, more *pallid*, more flimsy than English primroses. They lack some of the full wonder of the northern flowers. One tends to overlook them, to turn to the great, solemn-faced purple violets that rear up from the bank, and above all, to the wonderful little towers of the grape-hyacinth.

This is the time, in March, when the sloe is white and misty in the

如今，已是三月了，到了花朵竞相开放的时节了。在其他那些朝向阳光的溪流边，荆棘丛生，藜芦柔弱却不屈地挺过了整个冬季，就在这儿，一簇簇白色的报春花豁然开放了，它们开遍了整个灌木丛，蔓延到了溪水边。但跟英国报春花比起来，它们似乎显得更柔弱，更苍白，更单薄些。似乎也不如阿尔卑斯山北部的花朵那般让人感到惊艳。人们往往会忽视它们的存在，而将目光投向那些河岸边美丽庄严的紫罗兰，更或是那曼妙的麝香兰的小花塔。

三月时节，溪边灌木丛中白色的野李子花朦朦胧胧，斜坡上独自迎风

brier *n.* 荆棘；野蔷薇（丛）　　　　　bramble *n.* 荆棘；有刺灌木
hellebore *n.* <植>藜芦属植物　　　　　pallid *adj.* 苍白的

hedge-tangle by the stream, and on the slope land the peach tree stands pink and alone. The *almond* blossom, silvery pink, is passing, but the peach, deep-toned, bluey, not at all *ethereal*, this reveals itself like flesh, and the trees are like isolated individuals, the peach and the *apricot*. It is so conspicuous and so individual, that pink among the coming green of spring, because the first flowers that emerge from winter seem always white or yellow or purple. Now the *celandines* are out, and along the edges of the pond, the big, sturdy, black-purple anemones, with black hearts.

The daisies are out too, in sheets, and they are too red-mouthed. The first ones are big and handsome. But as March goes on, they dwindle to bright little things, like tiny buttons, clouds of them

---

的桃树一片粉红。杏花时期已过，银粉色的花朵也落了；桃子披上了深蓝色外衣，看起来一点也不轻灵，但却是本色出演；这时，桃树和杏树看起来真是各领风骚。告别冬季，初开的花朵一般都是白色、黄色或者紫色，所以，桃树所拥有的一片粉红，在此时的绿意盎然中，就显得颇为惹眼和别致。瞧，白屈菜也破土而出了。在湖边，高大强壮、紫黑色的海葵正高昂着头，露出它那黑色的花蕊。

雏菊也成片成片地开放了，红艳艳地惹人爱。初开的花又大又漂亮。随着三月逐渐过去，后开的花看上去就像一种如小纽扣般亮丽的小东西，一个个聚在一起。这意味着夏天即将到来。

---

almond *n.* 杏树

apricot *n.* 杏；杏树

ethereal *adj.* 灵气的；轻飘的

celandine *n.* 〈植〉白屈菜

together. That means summer is nearly here.

In some places there are odd yellow *tulips*, slender, spiky and Chinese-looking. They are very lovely, pricking out their dulled yellow in slim spikes. But they too soon lean, expand beyond themselves, and are gone like an illusion.

And when the tulips are gone, there is a moment's pause, before summer. Summer is the next move.

In the pause towards the end of April, when the flowers seem to *hesitate*, the leaves make up their minds to come out. For some time, at the very ends of the bare boughs of fig trees, *spurts* of pure green have been burning like cloven tongues of green fire vivid on the tips

---

在有些地方，你还能看到一些零落各处的、修长的、有穗的郁金香，展示着它们那别样的中式魅力，细长的穗尖上闪耀着的亮亮的黄色，甚是可爱。但很快地，它们也会变得孱弱起来，日渐无力，最后消失不见，一切恍若幻象。

随着郁金香的离去，花朵们都进入了夏日到来前的短暂休息期。夏日，就要来了。

在临近四月底的短暂休息期中，花朵们还在迟疑的时候，叶子们已经决意出头了。那段时间里，在原本光秃秃的无花果枝条上，尖端突然冒出了一抹抹嫩绿，像枝状大烛台上那生动的绿色小火舌似的燃烧起来。现

---

tulip *n.* 郁金香
spurt *n.* 喷出；涌出

hesitate *v.* 犹豫；踌躇

of the candelabrum. Now these spurts of green spread out, and begin to take the shape of hands, feeling for the air of summer. And tiny green figs are below them, like glands on the throat of a goat.

Now the *aspens* on the hill are all remarkable with the *translucent membranes* of blood-veined leaves. They are gold-brown, but not like autumn, rather like thin wings bats when like birds—call them birds—they wheel in clouds against the setting sun, and the sun glows through the stretched membrane of their wings, as through thin, brown-red stained glass. This is the red sap of summer, not the red dust of autumn.

在，这抹绿意延伸开来，已变成了小手的形状，感触着夏日的气息。小小的绿色无花果悬在下面，看起来就好像山羊喉中的腺。

现在，山坡上的白杨树格外地引人注目，因为它的叶脉上好似覆盖着一层半透明状的薄膜。叶子是金棕色的，并不是秋天的那种黄色，像是薄翼的蝙蝠，又好似鸟儿——我们就称其为鸟儿吧——它们在落日余晖映衬下的云层中翻飞，阳光照射在双翼伸展开的薄膜上，就像是照过了薄薄的棕红色的彩绘玻璃。这是属于夏日的红色汁液，并不同于秋日落叶遍地时的那种红色。

aspen *n.* 白杨
membrane *n.* 薄膜

translucent *adj.* 半透明的

The cherry tree is something the same, but more *sturdy*. Now, in the last week of April, the cherry blossom is still white, but waning and passing away: it is late this year, and the leaves are clustering thick and softly copper in their dark blood-filled glow. It is queer about fruit trees in this district. The pear and the peach were out together. But now the pear tree is a lovely thick softness of new and glossy green, vivid with a tender fullness of apple-green leaves, gleaming among all the green of the landscape, the half-high wheat, *emerald*, and the grey olive, half-invisible, the browning green of the dark *cypress*, the black of the evergreen oak, the rolling of the heavy green puffs of the stone-pines, the flimsy green of small peach and almond trees, the sturdy young green of horse-chestnut. So

---

　　樱桃树和白杨树属于相似的树种，不过更加强壮些。如今，已是四月份的最后一个星期了，白色的樱桃花依然高挂枝头，只是日渐柔弱，不久便将归入尘土：今年的时节来得晚了，树叶密密地，团团簇簇，深红色的光辉中映透着柔亮的古铜色。此处的果树比较奇特。梨花和桃花会同时开放。绿色遍野：长了一半的翠绿的麦子，犹抱琵琶半遮面的灰绿色的橄榄，深棕绿色的柏树，黑绿色的长青橡树，那翻滚着浓绿枝团的石松，浅绿色的小桃树和杏树以及强壮的有着新绿色的七叶树。种种绿色中，梨树清新亮丽的绿最为惹眼，它是那么可爱，那么浓重，又是那么轻柔，像苹果树绿色的叶子那般柔和饱满，鲜明生动。真是绿色的海洋啊！一片一片的，像斜斜的桌面，像浑圆的臂膀，像羽毛，像矮树丛，像直立的灌木。

---

sturdy *adj.* 强健的；结实的　　　　　　　　emerald *adj.* 翠绿色的
cypress *n.* 柏树

many greens, all in flakes and shelves and tilted tables and round shoulders and plumes and shaggles and uprisen bushes, of greens and greens, sometimes *blindingly* brilliant at evening, when the landscape looks as if it were on fire from inside, with greenness and with gold.

In the wood, the scrub-oak is only just coming uncrumpled, and the pines keep their hold on winter. They are wintry things, stone-pined. At Christmas, their heavy green clouds are richly beautiful. When the cypresses rise their tall and naked bodies of dark green, and the *osiers* are vivid red-orange, on the still blue air, and the land is lavender; then, in mid-winter, the landscape is most beautiful in colour, surging with colour.

绿色带着绿色，绿色连着绿色，当这整片的风景都好像从内部燃起来火来，绿色和金色相交融的时候，夜晚里偶尔望向这片绿色，也会觉得光彩夺目。

在林间冬日里，矮栎树尚没有倒下，松树也保持着自己原有的身姿，它们都是冬季植物，属于石松之类的。圣诞节时，它们团团的浓绿色更显得妩媚多姿。每当在宁静蔚蓝的空气中，柏树裸露出自己挺拔的、墨绿色的枝干，柳树展现出自己明艳的红橘色，大地蒙上一层淡紫色时，隆冬时节就来临了，此时的世界总是异彩纷呈，波光流转。

---

blindingly *adv.* 炫目地；显而易见地　　　　osier *n.* 柳条；柳树

Not that this week is flowerless. But the flowers are a little lonely things, here and there: the early purple *orchid*, *ruddy* and very much alive, you come across occasinally, then the little groups of bee-orchids, with their ragged concerted indifference to their appearance. Also there are the huge bud-spikes of the *stout*, thick-flowering pink orchid, huge buds like fat ears of wheat, hard-purple and splendid. But already odd grains of the wheat-ear are open, and out of the purple hangs the delicate pink rag of floweret. Also there are very lovely and choice cream-cloured orchids with brown spots on the long and delicate lip. These grow in the more moist places, and have exotic tender spikes, very rare-seeming. Another orchid is a little, pretty yellow one.

在这一星期里，花还是有的，但都是四处散开，弱小孤独的。偶然间，你便会看到它们：提前开放的紫兰花，面色红润，充满生机；小小的一簇簇的蜜蜂兰，步调一致，孤傲冷艳；还有那高举着硕大花苞穗的粉兰花，结结实实，缀满花瓣，硕大的花苞穗好似饱满的麦穗，闪耀着深紫色的光，缤纷异常；零零散散地，有些谷物的麦穗也开花了，紫色中点缀着粉红娇艳的朵朵小花；当然，还有那可爱的、精致的米色兰花，细长娇嫩的花蕊上跳跃着棕色的斑点，它们适宜生长在潮湿的环境中，常长有奇特的、不常见的柔嫩花穗；另一株兰花，则是小巧的、亮黄色的那种。

---

orchid *n.* 兰花   ruddy *adj.* 红润的
stout *adj.* 强壮的；结实的

By May, the nightingale will sing an unbroken song, and the discreet, barely *audible* Tuscan *cuckoo* will be a little more audible. Then the lovely pale-lilac *irises* will come out in all their showering abundance of tender, proud, spiky bloom, till the air gleam with mauve, and a new crystalline lightness will be everywhere. There will be tufts of iris everywhere, arising up proud and tender. When the rose-coloured wild *gladiolus* is mingled in the corn, and love-in-the-mist opens blue: in May and June, before the corn is cut.

But as yet is neither May nor June, but the end of April, the pause between spring and summer, the nightingale singing uninterrupted, the bean-flowers dying in the bean-fields, the bean-perfume passing with spring, the little birds hatching in the nests, the olives pruned,

---

五月到来后，夜莺的歌声愈加优美婉转，就连托斯卡纳杜鹃那难得一闻的歌声也变得清晰起来。接着，可爱的、淡紫色的鸢尾花便纷纷冒了出来，到处都是，那么柔美，那么骄傲，炫耀着它那穗状的花，直到空气中都弥漫着淡紫色，直到那清新透亮的淡雅之感四散开来。鸢尾花花开遍野，一丛丛，一簇簇，骄傲的，柔美的。五六月间，玉米收割还早，玫瑰色的野生剑兰会长到玉米地里，黑种草绽放出蓝色的花。

但现在还不到五月或六月，还只是四月底，是春夏之间的间隙，夜莺在婉转地歌唱，豆地里的豆花逐渐枯萎，豆香随着春天远去的脚步也慢慢

---

audible *adj.* 听得见的
iris *n.* 鸢尾花

cuckoo *n.* 布谷鸟；杜鹃
gladiolus *n.* 剑兰

and the vines, the last bit of late ploughing finished, and not much work to hand, now, not until the peas are ready to pick, in another two weeks or so.

So the change, the endless and rapid change. In the sunny countries, the change seems more vivid, and more complete than in the grey countries. In the grey countries, there is a grey or dark permanency, over whose surface passes change *ephemeral*, leaving no real mark.

But in the sunny countries, change is the reality and permanence is artificial and a condition of imprisonment. Hence, to the northerner, the phenomenal world is essentially tragical, because it is *temporal* and must cease to exist. Its very existence implies ceasing to exist,

消失不见了，小鸟在巢里孵蛋，橄榄树已被修剪好，葡萄也已经过了最后一道晚耕；大约两个星期后才能采摘豌豆，现在手边的活已经不多了。

这就是变化，永无休止的快速的变化。阳光明媚的区域，变化似乎更为鲜明，比在少见阳光的区域来得更加彻底。少见阳光的区域，似乎永远是灰蒙蒙、阴沉沉的。表面发生的变化只是一瞬间的事，不会留有任何痕迹。

然而，在阳光明媚的区域里，变化是一种现实，而永久则是虚饰的，象征着一种禁锢。因此，对北部的人们来说，他们所感知到的世界，本质上是令人悲伤的，因为那世界是短暂的，是注定要消失的。世界的存在本

ephemeral *adj.* 生命短暂的　　　　　　　temporal *adj.* 暂存的

and this is the root of the feeling of tragedy.

But to the southerner, the sun is so dominant that shadow, or dark, is only merely relative: merely the result of something getting between one and the sun.

In the human race, the one thing that is always there is the shining sun, and dark shadow is an accident of *intervention*.

For my part, if the sun always shine, and always will shine, in spite of millions of clouds of words. In the sunshine, even death is sunny. And there is no end to the sunshine.

That is why the rapid change of the Tuscan spring is *utterly* free, for me, of any senses of tragedy. The sun always shines. It is our fault if we don't think so.

身也预示了它未来的消亡，这就是人们悲伤的根源所在。

而对于南部的人们来说，阳光是十分重要的，阴影或黑暗仅仅是相对的：仅仅是因某物出现在人和太阳之间而产生的现象罢了。

对人类而言，有一样东西是永恒存在的，那就是闪耀的太阳，黑暗或阴影只是一种意外，一种干扰。

对我来讲，虽然众说纷纭，但太阳却一直照耀着我们，并将永远照耀着我们。在阳光下，就连死亡也充满着阳光。阳光是无尽的。

托斯卡纳的春天新旧更替，变幻无穷，我却并不因此感到甚至一丝一毫的悲伤，这就是因由所在。阳光是永远闪耀着的。若没有认识到这一点，这就是我们的不对了。

---

intervention *n.* 干涉；干预 　　　　　　　　utterly *adv.* 全然；完全地

38

Tribute to Dogs

— George Graham Vest

Gentlemen of the Jury:

The best friend a man has in the world may turn against him and become his *enemy*. His son or daughter that he has reared with loving care may prove ungrateful. Those who are nearest and dearest to us, those whom we trust with our happiness and our good name may become *traitors* to their faith. The money that a man has,

狗的礼赞

——乔治·格雷厄姆·维斯特

陪审团先生们：

即便是最好的朋友，也会和自己反目成仇。即便是自己含辛茹苦养育的儿女，也会忘恩负义。即便是以我们的幸福和忠贞相托的至近至亲的爱人，也会背信诺言。拥有的钱财也有散尽的时候。当我们最需要钱的时候，它却从我们身边不胫而走。一个人的声誉可能会因为计

---

enemy n. 敌人

traitor n. 叛徒

he may lose. It flies away from him, perhaps when he needs it most. A man's reputation may be sacrificed in a moment of ill-considered action. The people who are prone to fall on their knees to do us honor when success is with us, may be the first to throw the stone of *malice* when failure settles its cloud upon our heads.

The one absolutely unselfish friend that man can have in this selfish world, the one that never deserts him, the one that never proves ungrateful or *treacherous* is his dog. A man's dog stands by him in prosperity and in poverty, in health and in sickness. He will sleep on the cold ground, where the wintry winds blow and the snow drives *fiercely*, if only he may be near his master's side. He will kiss the hand that has no food to offer. He will lick the wounds and sores

划不周顷刻间被葬送。当成功与我们相伴时，那些五体投地敬仰我们的人，也许在失败的阴云笼罩在我们头上时，第一个对我们投井下石。

在这个自私自利的世界里，对人类绝对无私、不离不弃、感恩戴德、忠贞不渝的，就是他的狗了。无论是贫贱富贵，还是疾病健康，它都守在主人的身边。只要有主人在身边，哪怕是寒风刺骨大雪纷飞，它都会睡在冰冷的土地上。它会亲吻没有食物可给的双手。它会用舌头舔去遭遇世界冷遇后带来的创伤和苦痛。当沦为乞丐的主人熟睡时，它就守护在主人的身旁，如同王子一般。当所有的朋友都离他而去时，只有狗会留下来。当

malice *n.* 恶意　　　　　　treacherous *adj.* 背信弃义的；奸诈的
fiercely *adv.* 凶猛地；狂怒地

that come in encounters with the roughness of the world. He guards the sleep of his pauper master as if he were a prince. When all other friends desert, he remains. When riches take wings, and reputation falls to pieces, he is as constant in his love as the sun in its journey through the heavens.

If fortune drives the master forth, an *outcast* in the world, friendless and homeless, the faithful dog asks no higher *privilege* than that of accompanying him, to guard him against danger, to fight against his enemies. And when the last scene of all comes, and death takes his master in its embrace and his body is laid away in the cold ground, no matter if all other friends pursue their way, there by the *graveside* will the noble dog be found, his head between his *paws*, his eyes sad, but open in alert watchfulness, faithful and true even in death.

主人钱财散尽、一败涂地时，它对主人的爱如同日月青天，亘古不变。

　　如果命运对主人下逐客令，主人流落四方，没有朋友，无家可归，只有这条狗忠心耿耿地陪伴着他，别无他求，为他站岗防哨抵御危险，为他奋勇战斗反抗敌人。人生落幕时，主人与死亡拥抱，他的尸体被埋放在冰冷的地下。不管主人的朋友是否各寻他路四处散去，坟墓前只见这条高贵的狗。它的头趴在前爪之间，眼睛充满着悲伤，但仍然警觉地守卫着。就这样，忠贞不渝直到死亡。

---

outcast　*n.*　被抛弃者
graveside　*n.*　坟墓边

privilege　*n.*　特权
paw　*n.*　爪子